GUIDING SPIRITS

Doug Bookout & Friends

PUBLISHING HISTORY:

First Edition

Copyright © 2020 Douglas E. Bookout

Library of Congress: 1-8784727161

All Rights Reserved

ISBN: 978-1-09831-689-1

Published By: BookBaby Publishing

All Photographs by Doug Bookout unless specified

℘

"Come here,

Drink a lot,

Do bad things,

Don't get caught"

Mark Pentone, Blues Guitarist

New Orleans LA

ACKNOWLEDGEMENTS:

Sidney Smith & Haunted History Tours for the years of inspiration, support and opportunity. I wouldn't be living this dream if it wasn't for you.

Jonathan Weiss for being not only a fantastic mentor, and a role model, but a good friend. You, good sir, have definitely left a mark.

Drew Cothern for the amazing Artwork, not only on this book, but on the Dead Frenchmen Tour as well. You are one multi-talented MoFo.

To my wife Toni. My best friend, the love of my life, my support system, my inspiration, and my rock. I couldn't have done any of this without you. Nor would I have wanted to.

TABLE OF CONTENTS

ANECDOTES

ഇൽ•ൽക

PREFACE

What you're holding in your hands is a very different kind of New Orleans ghost and true tales story book. Instead of covering the stories that we relate on our tours, stories of past hauntings and atrocities in New Orleans history. We're giving you our first person accounts, as New Orleans ghost tour guides, of what we've seen and experienced on our tours, in the bars, the streets, the restaurants and in the hotels throughout the city. Oftentimes while in the process of relating those tour stories.

These encounters can range from funny, to spooky, to downright terrifying. Some are paranormal and some are not. But they still haunt us, nonetheless. And we're laying it out here, just for you.

I'm also extremely fortunate enough to work with some of the pre-eminent industry professionals. People I have known and respected for years, if not decades. And not just for their trade craft, but also for who they are, deep down, where it counts. Some of them have graciously agreed to join me in this labor of love and share some of their favorite stories, vignettes and anecdotes as well. So turn down the lights, pull up the covers, or get cozy in your favorite chair, perhaps along with your favorite New Orleans cocktail, and join us for Guiding Spirits – The Haunting Experiences of a New Orleans Tour Guide.

INTRODUCTION

Ahhhhh, that new Tour Guide smell. Freshly minted. Bursting with excitement, a slight tinge of whiskey, and paddle boat loads of information to share. That was me in April of 2016. I remember how proud I was when I passed the proctored test and received my official tour guide license from the City of New Orleans. I was now a culture bearer, a liaison, a representative of the city that I loved, proudly wrapped in Purple, Green and Gold, holding a cocktail aloft and beckoning others to join me on a journey through the naughty bits of New Orleans history.

For me, ladies and gentlemen, this was an achievement. The culmination of over a decade of day dreams, labor and planning to pursue my retirement bucket list with friends and adopted family in the City that Care Forgot. And I planned on giving it my all, because this is, as it is appropriately coined by Jason Berry, a "City of a Million Dreams". An old historical city where you can re-create and re-define yourself like no other place on the planet. As long as you're not too concerned about money, that is. And that's because the wages here, well, they're pretty much stuck in the past as well. But I digress.

In retrospect, after more than four years, I can honestly tell you, nothing in my background up to that point; no military or civilian law enforcement experience, no 30 plus years in the DoD Military Industrial Complex, no taking grandkids to Target while they were potty training, could prepare me for the monumental task of leading up to twenty-eight somewhat inebriated and wide eyed tourists through the labyrinth of the French Quarter on a Saturday night ghost tour. I mean, seriously. At times I thought I must have lost my mind. I like to joke that sometimes my life was easier when all I had to worry about was national security.

But you know what? I absolutely love it and wouldn't trade this experience for anything in the world! I get to live out my retirement drinking, costuming and sharing amazing stories with some really cool people in the best city on the planet. What a ride! And a privilege.

In general, a tour is an unspoken contract between the guide and their patrons. You come on my tour and I'm going to provide you with two hours of information and entertainment pertinent to the subject at hand. I'll take you to a location, tell you a story, give you details, answer questions, make you laugh (hopefully) and then I'll move you along to the next stop.

We'll lather, rinse and repeat that process several times until we successfully reach the end of the tour, be it in a museum, a historic battlefield or a posh neighborhood of the rich and famous. Oh, and if the planets align properly, you'll tip me at the end.

Now, imagine doing that in the middle of a full blown raucous party, with brass bands, and street musicians, with amplified sound, performing at various intervals along your tour route. Panhandlers busking for tips or cigarettes, drunk frat bros yelling obscenities, and cars, with monster sub woofers, rolling past your group along with every other bright and shiny object imaginable as your competition. Now you're starting to get a little glimpse of what we deal with on a frequent, almost daily, basis.

Couple that outside sensory overload of activity with disruptive people actually on your tour, who have decided to violate that aforementioned contract of listening, who have been drinking since noon (it's now 8pm) and want to interrupt, tell their stories, have a marital crisis, or show their boobs. Yes, both of husband and wife. And now you're starting to get the full picture.

Tour guides in New Orleans are freaking rock stars.

They, day in and day out, deal with situations most city police departments would have a hard time handling, and, all the while, with charm, wit, maturity and professionalism. Well, most of the time. As such, I am honored to be counted as one of their number.

So my goal, with this book, is to give us all a little spotlight, shine some recognition and provide a platform with which to share some of our own personal stories and experiences, both paranormal and anecdotal.

We're not going to detail the stories we tell on our tours. There are plenty of books out there that already do a fine job of that. And honestly, we'd rather just have you come visit and take our tours and immerse yourself in the full experience.

In my opinion there's nothing better than hearing a scary story or gruesome tale right on the property on which it occurred. There's a tangible energy in that experience like no other, because this city has a vibe, a hum, an atmosphere, like no other place on the planet. It's a place where it's easy to believe that magic still exists and dreams can still come true. It's intoxicating.

But beware, there's also a dark undercurrent to the city as well. It can pull you in and drag you down, as we've seen time and time again. Sadly, not all stories have a happy ending, in this gritty city. But that's the allure, isn't it? It's the seductive draw that makes people want to, as Blues guitarist Mark Pentone says, "come here, drink a lot, do bad things, don't get caught". I'm game. How about you?

THE BOURBON ORLEANS HOTEL
717 Orleans St.

I've always had an affinity for twisted tales and a fascination with the otherworldly. Having grown up in the 60's and 70's on TV shows like Night Gallery, The Twilight Zone and Dark Shadows and books like Red Skelton's Favorite Ghost Stories, The Legend of Sleepy Hollow and the tales of Edgar Allen Poe, the pull of the paranormal and macabre has always beckoned.

My siblings and I also believe that our Mom was a naturally gifted sensitive. She could sense things that others couldn't and often see things, through her maternal connection, that happened to us miles away. Later, when we got home, she would question us "did you go back and get your change at the McDonald's counter?", or comment, "I see you found your keys". These occurrences became common place in my early years, but then, as I grew up and moved away, the demands of career and family loomed large and that connection and fascination with the paranormal fell away. That was, until my first trip to New Orleans.

A single orb drifts to the right of "Touchdown Jesus" during a full moon over St. Louis Cathedral

It was January 2004 and I was scheduled to speak at a conference at Eglin AFB. While planning my trip I happened to notice that New Orleans was only about a four hour drive from the base. Having never been there I requested some time off after the conference and flew my wife Toni out to meet me for an extended weekend. We had no idea that this little trip would forever change our lives.

The Bourbon Orleans Hotel is located right in the heart of the French Quarter at the intersection of Bourbon and Orleans streets. Its grand ballroom was once host to the infamous Quadroon Balls in the early to mid-1800s and the Bourbon Street side was once home to first New Orleans opera house. It's also very haunted.

The second night into our stay was when we had our first strange incident in our room. Getting ready for an evening out in the Quarter, we had laid our outfits out on the bed and my wife jumped in the shower while I shaved at the sink. That's when I heard a noise from the bedroom.

It sounded like something fell over. Drying my face, I walked into the suite to find our clothes thrown all around the room and our suitcase turned upside down. I was dumbfounded.

We were on the sixth floor and the only way in or out of the room was through the locked door right next to the bathroom. There was no way anyone could have gotten past me without being seen. When my wife got out of the shower I showed her what happened and, of course, she thought I was playing a joke on her and trying to scare her. I assured her that was not the case, but I'm not sure I convinced her, until a few days later.

If you're not aware, the Mardi Gras season always begins on 12th night, or Three Kings Day, which always falls on January 6th, twelve days after the birth of Christ. Since we were there in late January, as luck would have it, we were attending our first Mardi Gras season during our first visit, which was really exciting.

Of course the bead trade was in full effect at that time, so each night we ventured out we would get showered with beads from the balconies above Bourbon Street.

Our first night out we caught quite the haul and I had about 3 pictures left to burn on a roll of film. Once we got back to the room I had my wife throw the all of beads on so I could get a few bead trophy snaps and finish the roll.

The next day we had them developed at the place across the street and when I went in to pick them up, the owner called me over to show me an anomaly in a few of my pictures. Turns out they were the three I had shot the night before in the hotel room. In each shot, there was a serpentine white mist in front of my wife, moving through the picture. It was translucent in some areas and opaque in others.

The developer said "this appears to be a solid object moving through the frame. It's in a different location in each shot and doesn't appear in any of the photos on the roll before this." Another interesting aspect of the "object" was that it was covering my wife's body, regardless of how it moved through the frame. The roll I shot after that, at locations throughout the city, never showed the same anomaly, but we do believe we figured out the reason why.

On our last night in town, and intrigued by the weird goings on in our room, we decided to take a Ghost Tour. Our Guide, Julia, was fantastic and during the tour, I began to feel that pull again, towards that long forgotten fascination with the paranormal. We stopped for our last story on the tour and lo and behold it was in front of our hotel, the Bourbon Orleans. There Julia told us a tale of the long ago Quadroon balls, and how a young lady named Henriette Delille, who was destined for that fate of Placage, or becoming the concubine of a rich Creole Gentleman, rejected that life and formed the first African American cloister of nuns known as The Sisters of the Holy Family.

At one point a rich entrepreneur by the name of Thomas Lafon became a patron of their work on behalf of orphaned children and in a gesture of great charity, purchased the ballroom for them to use as their convent. One nun, distraught over being disowned by her family for refusing to participate in the system of Placage, committed suicide by hanging herself in the convent, near the 600 series of rooms in the hotel. Our room. That's when the realization hit us. It was the Nun. She was not happy with our "farewell to the flesh" display of revelry in our room and this was her way of letting us know to mind our Ps and Qs during our stay.

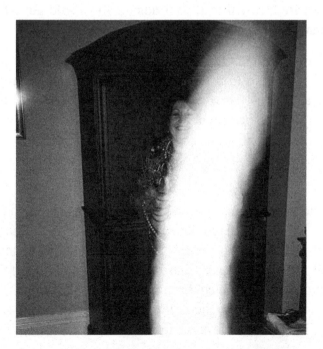

Bead Photo (Insert phallic ghost jokes here)

However, as fate would have it, that was not to be our last encounter with the Nun on the sixth floor. The next year, in February of 2005, we returned with friends to perform a renewal of vows ceremony at one of our favorite blues clubs. Of course, we had to stay at the Bourbon Orleans and requested a room in the same location as we had during our initial visit.

Our room had a small, stand-alone balcony the jutted out from the building, with the balconies for the adjacent rooms about 6 feet apart. We decided to have a small party in our room with some of our friends and spent several hours drinking and throwing beads off of our balcony to the revelers down below and to other guests in the adjoining balconies. At one point, probably around two AM, we all decided to call it a night, and I pushed two metal patio chairs out to the corners of the balcony so I could pull the double doors shut. I remember joking to my wife that we were probably keeping the Nun up and should head to bed. We had a good chuckle and fell off to sleep.

When I woke up the next morning I promptly pulled back the curtains from the double doors to find both patio chairs wedged securely against the doors on the balcony, in essence, sealing them shut. Remember, these doors open out, and before heading to bed I had to push them out to the far corners of the balcony so I could get the door to close.

I kind of freaked out. I mean, this was a free standing balcony, six feet away from the other balconies on either side and on the highest floor of the building. You would have had to have been Spiderman to have gotten up there.

Sadly, in my excitement, I forgot to take a picture before rushing to push open the doors, which was quite a chore. Those chairs were heavy iron cast and were difficult to move.

I can assure you, there were no more jokes about the Nun after that. We continued to stay at the Bourbon Orleans for every visit until the fall of 2011 when we bought our first house in the city and plotted our retirement. We always remained respectful and never had another incident at *that* location again. Unbeknownst to us, we were just getting started.

ANECDOTE: FAMILY REUNION

My grandfather checking in on our family reunion, which was held at the property on which he passed. Cherryville, NC. 2003.

Family Reunion Photo

2

THE DUNGEON
738 Toulouse Street

The Dungeon is a legendary Goth rock metal bar, established in 1969, and famous for its dark music, creepy S&M themed atmosphere and risqué behavior by its patrons. It is literally my favorite bar in the French Quarter. Word got out fast in the 70's and soon, locals, tourists, movie stars and some of the greatest bands in rock and roll history flocked to the Dungeon during their visits to New Orleans. I mean, we're talking the likes of Queen, Zeppelin, Heart, Lou Reed, Motely Crue, and David Bowie, just to name a few.

There's even a story about the ghost of a young bartender who frequently haunts the bar who committed suicide after Jimmy Paige stole away his smoking hot girlfriend, Patricia. This allegedly happened right under his nose, during one of his shifts at the Venus bar in 1975. Amongst other creepy activities, such as standing where the security cameras can see him, this ghost takes strong exception to people playing Zeppelin on the juke box downstairs. One day I decided to put that story to the test. I'll share the results with you in a moment.

Understandably, in a bar like this, in a city like New Orleans, sometimes that dark mix can result in tragedy, and over the years the bar has been the flash point for a few murders, suicides and other various and sundry bad things throughout its storied history. This all, quite fittingly, just adds to the mystique.

That's one reason why current bands still keep that legacy of rock and roll patronage alive when they're in town. While doing tours, or just afterwards, I've walked in to find members of the Foo Fighters, Alien Ant Farm, Evanescence, Rage Against the Machine, Lindsey Stirling, Machine Gun Kelly, Post Malone, Matt O'Ree Band, Maid of Orleans and Pussy Wolf, reposing in the shadows.

With Rachel Lockett and Terry Corso – Alien Ant Farm

But, let's get back to that young bartender who committed suicide and still inhabits the bar. As I mentioned, this ghost often appears upstairs in the security cameras, standing there, with his head down, arms by his side, reclaiming his territory and, in essence, saying "no matter what happened, I'm still here." Downstairs, he harasses patrons who have the audacity to play Zeppelin tunes on the jukebox. When I had just started taking my tours there, probably the summer of 2017, I heard the story and decided to put this claim to the test. I showed up early one evening as Rachel (the bartender) and Drew (the Door Guy) were just opening up. We were the only three in the bar at the time, so I walked over, put a dollar in the juke box and selected three Zeppelin tunes.

I sat back down, ordered a drink and conversed with Rachel for a few minutes, when suddenly, someone poked me in the back, right between the shoulder blades, hard. So hard, in fact, that it really pissed me off, because, well, it hurt. I wheeled around expecting to find Drew standing there grinning, messing with me, and there was no one. Empty. I was the only living person on the patron side of the bar. And Drew? He was standing outside in the courtyard smoking a cigarette.

Rachel, registering what had just occurred, leaned against the bar with an amused "I told you so" smile and said "welcome to the Dungeon, Doug." So, that was my introduction to the spirits at the Dungeon. As disconcerting as that was, it would do nothing to prepare me for what was to come next.

About six months after my initial experience I was conducting a tour on a Sunday evening with a full tour of 28 people. People love this haunted pub crawl. I had just finished telling my group about the notorious 2003 Vampire murder, perpetrated by a couple who called themselves "Never & Worry". They met and seduced their victim at, you got it, The Dungeon. We filed into the bar, as usual, and immediately took over both levels of the establishment. The place isn't that big.

We had been there for about 10 minutes when the upstairs bouncer brought one of my tour patrons over to me at the Venus bar, where I was chatting with a friend. The girl looked to be mid-twenties, blonde, and scared out of her mind. Apparently something had occurred that really shook her up. I asked her if she was okay and she responded; "I want to leave right now". I asked her what happened and again, she responded "I just want to get out of here. Right now." Fair enough. At that point her husband had joined us with two drinks in his hands and a very perplexed look on his face. The bouncer, her husband, and I, escorted her shakily down the stairs and out to the courtyard where she sat down on the bench that looks like a torture rack. We got her a bottle of water, and that's when the story began to unfold.

They were hanging out in the upstairs section known as the Sound Bar, leaning against the wall next to the cage you can dance in, complete with shackles (yes, really) when a spot opened at the bar and the husband decided to go get them drinks. She was causally leaning with her back against the wall, watching the other patrons, when suddenly someone, or something, grabbed her hair from behind and pulled her head back against the wall. Now remember, she's leaning against a solid brick wall on the second floor of a building. At first she thought her hair got caught or tangled in something.

Reaching back to free herself, she quickly realized that her head was flush against the wall and whatever was holding on to her, was, impossibly, on the other side.

She struggled to free herself and is unable to do so. She screamed for her husband, who is at bar about five feet away, but his back is to her and the music is loud, so he can't hear her. Panicked, she begins slapping at the wall with both hands and yelling let me go!

The bouncer sees her from across the room and thinks she's having a seizure of some kind. He walks over and lays his hand on her shoulder, asking if she's okay. Immediately, upon making that contact, she breaks free… and runs, as fast as she can, across the room towards the stairs. She actually ran so fast the bouncer said that she bounced off of the stairwell wall at the top of the stairs and fell back into the doorway of the bar. That's when he helped her up and brought her to me on the Venus side of the bar.

I have to admit, I was dumbfounded. I had never heard of anything like this happening before. Ashlee, one of the upstairs bartenders who had witnessed the whole incident, came down to check on her. And that's when I learned the story of the suicide girl.

With Ashlee & Drew Schmidt (Top) and Rachel Lockett and my wife
Toni - Halloween 2018

Apparently a young couple came to New Orleans with friends in 2005 to celebrate their new engagement.

At some point during their visit to the Dungeon, the girl realized that she couldn't find her fiancé. After checking up and down the bar, she finally approached the door guy with a picture of him on her phone and asked if he had seen him leave.

The door guy responded that he had, in fact, seen him leave with one of her girlfriends about 20 minutes earlier. Knowing that all her girlfriends were with her, she suddenly wanted to know who the skank was that her fiancé walked off with.

Checking the street around the bar and unable to locate him, she returned to the bar and continued to drink. Hard. And she waited, thinking that he would return. After quite a bit of time passed it was obvious that he was not coming back. Her friends convinced her to go back to the hotel and they would deal with "the asshole" in the morning and reluctantly she agreed. Sadly she was found the next morning having passed away in her sleep from taking too many sleeping pills. Her friends believed it was an accident, too much alcohol had clouded her judgement and she overdosed.

Now she returns, upon occasion, looking for the girl who stole her fiancé. And when she finds someone who fits the profile she acts out on them by pulling hair, tripping, poking and pushing. Even to the point of placing her hands on the backs of girls seated on the toilet in the ladies room.

Apparently supportive gestures from people nearby, such as the upstairs bouncer, is what breaks the contact (I know, hard to do in a bathroom). From that night on I have generally issued a word of caution to my tour patrons prior to entering. Most of my blonde female patrons make a brunette or ginger sandwich with their friends during their stay. So far it has worked. Well, it did, until something entirely different happened in the summer of 2019. More on that in a later chapter.

Pray you don't have an encounter with the Suicide Girl while visiting The Dungeon.

One Saturday evening I was assigned a Haunted Pub Crawl with a group of 28 Human Resources professionals in town for a conference at the Convention Center. I felt pretty comfortable about this, seeing as I had worked closely with HR in my past life, so no problem, we're all professionals. Let's do this. I watched as newcomers were introduced to conference regulars, members were reunited and the mood was generally upbeat and positive. It was gonna be a good night.

I kicked off my tour, as usual, took them to our first stop and everyone was drinking and paying close attention to the stories. So far so good. After the second bar stop things started getting a little wonky. People who had just been introduced, maybe 40 minutes earlier, were starting to get pretty chummy with one another, if you get my drift.

By the third bar stop I literally had tour patrons asking where they could find hookers and blow. I'm not kidding. I was awarded the "worst tour guide ever" title by one lady for not assisting with their request. I mean, if you ask me personally, I might know a guy, but when I'm representing a company, sorry, not gonna happen.

Finally, after I finished my last story in front of what can best be described as a somewhat fully clothed orgy, I dragged everyone into the last bar. The tips were meagre, as you would expect from this type of group, but the Coup de Gras was when the lady who had dubbed me the "worst tour guide ever" came over and apologized. She tipped me $20 and said she was sorry she had been so snippy, but since her STD had flared up, it was really impacting her chances of getting laid during this trip. Then she smiled and offered to buy me a drink.

As you can imagine, I was dead! I offered my condolences for her broken lady parts with the just right amount of mourning, and got out of there as fast as humanly possible. So here's to you, my HR peeps, I see you! Respect! With all that buttoned down rule keeping, turns out you guys really know how to party!

3

THE PHARMACY MUSEUM
514 Chartres Street

The Pharmacy Museum. Hands down my favorite museum attraction in the Quarter, just brimming with visual history. This was the first registered pharmacy in the United States opened in 1823 by Dr. Louis Dufilho, a New Orleans native. From the moment you see the large glass urns filled with colored liquid in the apothecary windows, which were used to signal plague outbreaks, you'll be whisked back in time to a certainly simpler, yet more deadly time in New Orleans history. A time where yellow fever, cholera and malaria killed people each year like clockwork in the summer months. Where potions and various concoctions attempted to cure what ailed you, and where the rich would coat their medicines in silver and gold, not realizing they were ironically reducing the efficacy of the drugs meant to save their lives.

Oh, and once you see what passed for a catheter in the early 1800's you won't walk right for a week.

Photo by Tim Brunty

Note: Sadly, as I write this, the Covid-19 virus is hitting the city hard, disproportionately affecting the African American community. For a city who has grown used to tragedy, this situation sadly, feels all too familiar.

On our tours we tell the torrid tale of Dr. Joseph Dupas, an "opportunistic doctor" who, in the mid-1800s, used the plague outbreaks as cover for his nefarious deeds. He would have those who he deemed the lowest in New Orleans society, typically enslaved people, prostitutes and transients, kidnapped and brought to him so he could use them as test subjects for his experiments and procedures. These ghastly operations were usually performed in the entresol storage space above the apothecary on the first floor and always resulted in the death of the test subject, even if the "operation" was a success.

Dupas would generally bribe the death cart drivers to not only find these unfortunate souls for him, but also help him dispose of their remains once he was finished with them. For these services he paid them handsomely with money, drugs, alcohol. Whatever they desired. It also means that the carriage way on the side of the building figured prominently in his operation as the good doctor would raise and lower his victims through the entresol trap door.

Active hauntings on the property include white mists, moaning sounds, orbs, antiseptic smells, moving and displaced objects and the occasional apparition of a man descending the back stairs in a dark brown lab coat. The ghost of Dr. Dupas.

In the four years of doing tours at this location I've had quite a few standout occurrences. Most notably are those of frequent camera malfunctions while patrons are taking pictures down the carriageway. In the instances when patrons bring an actual camera, not a camera phone, to the location, they will experience issues with somewhat bizarre results regardless of whether digital or film. I've had patrons have their camera fail to take a picture down the carriageway, turn and shoot a perfect photo across the street and then turn back to have their camera fail again and again to capture an image down carriageway. I've watched time and again as patrons get white mists, orbs and what I can only describe as a spectral dispersal of energy in their photos. Allow me to share a couple of recent occurrences with you.

In October of 2019, during the Halloween, or Samhain, season, when we believe, as the Celts do, that the veil between the living and the dead is at its thinnest, the following images were captured during my tours.

The first image was taken by a local young man who brought his out of town friends on my Haunted Pub Crawl. He confessed to me at an earlier bar stop that he was a skeptic regarding the paranormal, but thought it would be fun for his friends. His tone changed significantly when he turned around from the carriage gate to show me the following image.

The trap door

The opaque ectoplasmic mist snaking down from above in this picture is actually coming down from the entresol trap door in the ceiling. The same trap door where Dr. Dupas would hoist and then later, lower his victims. Many viewers of this photo see the images of faces and skulls imbedded in the mist.

Three days later, I was with another tour group taking pictures down the carriageway, when a young lady startled and ran back from gate to the curb across the sidewalk.

I chuckled and asked her if a rat had run across the alley way, because that can happen quite a bit in this old port city. She looked at me wide eyed and said "No. I was taking pictures when this white mist started forming in the alley. With each picture I took it seemed to move closer to me. I felt like it was coming after me, so I ran."

The girl who ran to the curb

Two days after that occurrence the shades on the front doors were open, which is rare, so one lady pressed her camera against the glass so she could take pictures of the darkened interior. The first picture came out very clear, the second one, not so much. Then the third, clear again. I've included photos 1 and 2 below. Judge the results for yourself. Also, she was there alone as the group had already moved on.

No movement of the camera, no change in light, just a spectral discharge of energy that was there one second and gone the next.

White Mist - 2017

So please, come join me on one of my tours and when we arrive at the Pharmacy Museum, let's see what captures you.

We believe that spirits are curious about the living, especially when you're visiting their property, so they come to check you out to see what type of person you are and what you're saying about them. When they do, their energy can affect electronic devices and result in all these camera anomalies we experience. Because I encounter this quite often, my wife has given me the edict, "Do not bring this shit home with you." You'll better understand her concern after you read Chapter 13. This is why I wear a protection ring while on my tours, to keep them from hitching a ride home with me.

Fans (at center) meeting Matt & Eryn O'Ree at BMC

Next photo – Spirits come to Visit

A HAUNTED PUB CRAWL HIJACKING OF SORTS

Randy Walker

So this all happened on a pub crawl tour, a haunted pub crawl tour, to be precise. This can be a great tour at times. And at other times, not so much. This is a story of a not-so-great time, where I am in charge of guiding a bachelor party of five to four different bars in two hours. Before the tour even starts I know this might be a challenge. I have no idea how stupid things would get though.

Our first stop is relatively harmless. We enter this restaurant/bar on the corner of Bourbon and St Peter, and go upstairs to the 2nd floor bar to get drinks. So these guys order drinks, crack jokes and slap each other on the back and all that goofy fun. That's a good sign.

Being the professional tour guide that I am, I join in on the fun, grabbing a beer from the bartender and laughing along with the group acting like I'm just another member of their party. So far nothing bad.

After we get our first round of drinks, I lead my men to a secret room to tell the story. And that goes well too. They laugh at all the right parts, they listen well, gasp at the horror, and even curse at the worst of it. When I finish telling the story of the poor family who were burnt to a crisp in the fire of 1794, they give me a nice round of applause and I lead them downstairs to the exit and I'm thinking to myself:

Oh, this tour will be just fine.

But then, when we are back downstairs, heading outside again to continue to the next stop, I feel a tap on my shoulder and receive the first indicator that this group might be problematic.

"Hey bro," one of the guys says to me, "would it be cool for us to get another round of shots here before we head to the other place."

Now this is the sort of question I can't really say no to without coming across like a jerk, but I really want to say no to this. The next bar is only four blocks away, and I know when groups start going heavy on the drinking early in the tour... it'll only complicate things later. But what I'm I gonna do? I work for tips.

So they take their shots and we exit the restaurant/bar and start walking to the next one.

It's here, on this walk, where these guys start to annoy me. One of them, let's assume Gary, spots a discarded, half full beer can lying on the curb, and proceeds to run up and kick it as hard as he can, sending it crashing down the street. This is followed by a cry of:

"And the kick is gooooooooooood!"

I calmly, but firmly, tell him to please go pick up the can and throw it away, and not to do things like that again, because we're on a tour and I could get in trouble for something like that, plus it's not polite to the neighbors. That's when one of his buddies puts his arm around Gary's neck and answers for him.

"Aw, we're sorry. Gary just gets like that sometimes. He's a wild one. In fact, we are all a little wild, right guys?"

To which a small cacophony of hoots and hollers follow.

Ah yes, so wild, I think, kicking a can down the street, you bunch of James Deans you…

"Oh man, this guy is gonna hate us by the end of the tour!" one of the others says to his friends, like I'm not even there, " He's gonna remember us forever and he's gonna hate us!"

Hearing this makes me cringe.

If there is one statement that I can't stand that I get constantly from my different groups it is this. I'm convinced the only people who utter this phrase to a tour guide are those that have never worked in the service industry at all. Because those who have know one obvious fact about a job like this, you forget 99.9 percent of the people you serve. As soon as they leave your little world, you forget about them almost immediately. Maybe while you served them they annoyed you, maybe they were fine, maybe they made your day a little better. Maybe they made it a whole lot worse. It doesn't matter. As soon as they are gone they disappear from your mind. Only the very great and the very worst get any sort of residency in your brain, the rest vanish immediately. And at this point, I'm positive these jokers aren't qualifying for either position. But I don't bother explaining that. Instead I just give my standard answer:

"Ah no, you guys are fine. I've had way worse. I actually like you guys." (Did I mention I work for tips?)

Anyway, this renegade crew proceeds to rebel in the following ways:

-Slapping on the top of the occasional trash can as we walk down the sidewalk.

-making loud, lewd comments about the women in their lives back home (note: they   were silent about those that passed them by IRL though).

- shoving each other into gallery posts.

-asking one of the bartenders for her number (while the rest snicker loudly).

-making bad jokes while I tell stories.

- telling each other how much I hate them and will always remember them.

So all in all, this gang of five has devolved into your typical annoying-but-unmemorable pub crawl group, and that's fine. I'm not in a great mood, so it's irritating me more than it should, but it's fine.

On our third stop, we make it to May Bailey's, the one high class bar on the tour that has a delightful brothel story. And would you believe this? While I'm describing the brothel, and the women who work there, my group says things to each other like:

"Matt would go there everyday!"

"Eric would never leave!"

"Gary would get a job there!"

"(laughing) Would you guys stop? This tour guide is going to hate us forever!"

So yeah, still just your average pub crawl tour that, if I would have been in a more giving mood, might have even been a little fun. But as I said before, I am just not feeling it tonight, so I do what I always do when I'm working a tour and it's not going well. not feeling the vibe of the group.
I. get. through. It.
Sometimes that's the greatest weapon a tour guide has.
I raise my voice when they make their jokes and little comments and fight my way to the end of the story.
More than halfway through, I tell myself, only thirty minutes to go. Finally, I finish the third story, and we are on our way down Dauphine Street to our last stop. Now I have a tendency to hold my breath at this section of the tour, because it's the most sketchy area that we travel down. Up until that point, nothing bad has ever happened here during one of my tour, but you have a lot of drug dealers and other criminal elements that frequent the area. I have always felt that I had an unspoken agreement with this sketchy element of the quarter though, which is essentially:

You leave my group alone, I leave you alone.

That might have been wishful thinking, but in all my years doing this nothing bad had happened yet.

And then, as we are about to come up to Toulouse Street, I notice something strange. There's a man on a bike riding alongside me in the street. And he's got a big, stupid grin on his face, like the cat who ate the canary or whatever. And the stupid face with the stupid grin looks awfully familiar. But how would I know this guy? A friend from the neighborhood? A fellow service industry worker?

He rides past me as I'm trying to figure it out. And then, a lot of things happen at once:

- I hear my group behind me start laughing uproariously.

- I see a man who I recognize as being part of the sketchy element that I mentioned earlier running down the street toward us screaming profanely and furiously.

- I recall ten seconds earlier, as we were walking down the sidewalk, that I passed by a bicycle resting against a building wall, while two men discussed something in secret not five feet from the bike.

-Finally, I remember why that man with the stupid grin on his face riding the bike looked so familiar, it's one of the fucking five guys on my tour (let's say Gary).

Oh Jesus Christ, this is bad, I think to myself.

And as I'm processing all this, the running man passes us on the street, screaming again at the idiot who stole his bike, and I hear him clearly shout:

"I'm gonna kill you motherf---er!"

And by God, I believe him. With my whole heart I believe that he means those words. In this area, in the French Quarter, at night, I can safely say that people have been killed for less. And what really gets to me at this moment is the rest of the group behind me is dying of laughter. All four of them slapping their knees and holding on to each other for support as the chuckles vomit out of their drink holes.

"Oh f--king Gary man!"

"Gary's an animal!"

"Look at Gary go!"

In a panic, I turn to them and try to impress upon them how bad this situation is, telling them that they need to go grab their boy before something really bad happens. But their response is to only laugh harder and further praise of Gary's wild heart.

I turn my head back to the nightmare scenario unfolding in front of me, and find that it's only grown worse. What I haven't realized til now is that Gary is riding the stolen bike the wrong way down a one way street, and there's a car not too far away at all heading right for him whose driver seemed to have no idea Gary's pedaling toward him, or just doesn't care.

My mind tries to process this. Violent angry, death-threatening sprinting man on one side, oblivious speeding car on the other, "Wild Gary" in the middle. Simply put, it's the French Quarter sandwich from hell.

Of course, in situations such as these, your life goes into slow motion, and with each turn of the pedal I try to weigh my options here. Do I go after Gary myself and try to save him? Do I save time and just call the ambulance now? Do I just run away from this whole mess and claim the group ditched me after the third stop? None of these options are appealing, so I start thinking of how I'm going to explain this to my boss, when he learns that someone on my tour hijacked a vehicle and immediately got into one of the oddest traffic accidents/murders of all time.

And while I'm thinking on this, the group of jackals behind me are still giggling like children, and Gary is still joy riding, and both the angry man and the car are gaining steam, bearing down on him.

F--- my life, is all I can think.

Now, I don't know how much of this has been exaggerated over time in my head, but as I remember it, Gary's not ten feet away from the front bumper of the incoming car before the bike owner reaches him and throws a right handed haymaker at the left side of his head, causing him to slump over to the left, causing the bike to veer hard to the left so that both the bike and Gary miss the car completely (the car also may have slammed on the brakes at the last minute, but that's honestly not how I remember it. But if it didn't, why didn't the irate bike owner get run over by the car seconds later? These are the questions I have no answer to.)

I breathe a small sigh of relief, as at least Gary wasn't killed by a vehicle. However, my relief is very momentary, because the bike owner is hovering above him as he lays on the ground, with two balled up fists, echoing familiar threats of the recent past. This would have been bad enough, but the fact that Gary's on the ground laughing hysterically while looking up at the bike owner...well, I feel like this is an added insult to injury that does not help the situation. And of course, behind me, I hear the familiar calls of:

"F--king Gary man!"

"He's a legend!"

Even now, his friends make no effort to help their friend, or take the situation serious. This infuriates me so much, I almost want something bad to happen. Just so they will finally understand that you don't pull this dumb shit in the quarter, and if you do, you don't laugh it off like it's nothing, because it's not.

The next thing I know, I see the bike owner back on his bike, pedaling past us. Behind him, Gary is still on the ground, still laughing like a maniac. As the biker passes us, I see him turn to me with angry fucking eyes and say:

"And f--k you too."

Oh dear, I think, whatever deal we had before is over now...

Gary's friends finally run over to their fallen friend and help him up. All of them are laughing. Especially Gary.

"Gary, you're out of your mind, buddy!"

I quickly get them back on the sidewalk and march them a few blocks away before laying into them. I explain to them how dangerous that was. I explain how stupid that was. I explain that if they pull anything like that again, this fucking tour is over (some tour guides here will admonish me, saying if it was them, that would have been the end of the tour right then and there. I can't argue this, all I can say is I am a whore for tips, and in the back of my mind I'm hoping that this guilt trip will help with some major cash love at the end [spoiler alert- it didn't]).

I tell them all this, in my angry AND disappointed tour guide voice. When I'm done, one of the guys turns to his friends and says as if I'm not standing there:

"Oh man, this tour guide is gonna hate us forever by the end of the tour! He'll never forget how awful we were!"

Amidst their cackling, I can't help but finally agree with this sentiment. I will never forget how awful they are.

ANECDOTE: KARMA TAKES A TOUR – *Stella Salmen*

I have had all kinds of people on my tours. Some are believers, some are skeptics, but I hope all of them are at least a bit open minded and curious. I do my best to present things in a manner that, while not "converting" anyone, might make them at least question their idea of normal. On one tour, however, I believe I converted and entire group into believing in psychic energy.

While giving a tour presentation about the basic history of Voodoo, I had a group of people that decided they would disrupt my tour. OK, that happens frequently enough, but these people decided that they would NOT stop. They had balloons, loud music playing, clown make-up. (If you don't know New Orleans well, you might think this strange. Trust me, it is not.)

After several polite requests to kindly move on, they got rather nasty with me… then they did, indeed, proceed to walk further up the street, yelling foul insults at me. Again, these things happen. But this time it was more annoying than usual. I looked at my group, who were in awe that this had happened, and just smiled.

One man made a comment about how I really "kept my cool". I responded, not loudly, but in a low speaking voice that my entire group did hear, "I hope she breaks her ankle", followed with a rather sardonic smile.

At that precise moment, we hear a loud "Yelp" halfway down the block, as the woman at the back of the obnoxious group turns her ankle and falls in the street.

The look of shock on every face was simply precious.

I resumed the tour with, "Now, to continue with Voodoo…"

Best. Coincidence. Ever.

DEAD KIDS

Dead Kids. They absolutely terrify me. From the screaming boy in the Grudge, to the Grady Twins from The Shining and the tongue clucking little girl of Hereditary, if you're at a scary movie with me, that's when I'm coming out of my seat. REDRUM? Yeah. Fuck that.

Yet the city of New Orleans, where I live, is filled to the brim with ghost lore and the tales of dead children. It seems they are occupying practically every building in the French Quarter. Yay. So the next few chapters are dedicated to these young denizens of the after-life and their interactions with we earth bound souls. Some are innocent, some are tragic and some, like the tale I'm about to share with you, are wickedly mischievous.

One of my favorite ghost tales, ever, is a story we were told on our very first ghost tour in the city as we stood across Royal Street from the Andrew Jackson Hotel. Apparently, at one point in this properties fascinating history, it was a boarding school where five young boys tragically died in a fire and who still occupy the grounds, playing amongst the guests of the hotel. Watching them sleep. Touching their stuff.

The story we were told was of a young couple visiting from Texas in 2002. They checked into the hotel, excited about their visit to New Orleans, and promptly got to unpacking. The wife takes her toiletries to the bathroom and is startled to see a little boy standing in the bathroom. He's dressed in a shirt and overalls and appears to be about eight years old.

Astonished, she kneels before the little boy and asks;

"Sweetheart, are you lost?"

"Where's your family?"

The boy doesn't respond, just stands there stoically, staring right at her.

After a few additional attempts to talk to him, she tells him "Wait here, we'll find them."

With visions of Home Alone, she runs into the room, past her stupefied husband and grabs the phone. She shushes him as he's asking "what is going on and who were you talking to?" and begins talking to the desk clerk;

"There's a lost little boy in our room and I need you to help me find his family right away."

The Desk Clerk responds, nonchalantly; "Ma'am, just leave him alone and he'll go away."

She says "What? What do you mean he'll go away? His parents must be frantic!"

Again, the clerk calmly restates "Trust me. Just leave him alone and he'll go away. This happens quite often."

Suddenly it dawns on her. She's heard the stories, the ghosts of dead kids on the property. She abruptly hangs up the phone and grabs her camera from the dresser, runs into the bathroom and levels it at the little boy with the intention of taking his picture. He screws up his face in a little grimace, clearly unhappy, and disappears, instantly, before she can snap the shot.

She's stunned.

To the surprise of her husband, she decides she wants to stay, in that room. Her heart has been touched by that little boy and she desperately wants to make contact with him again. Her husband reluctantly agrees. It becomes kind of an obsession for her during their trip, her husband having to pry her away from the room to attend outside activities. But the face of that little boy keeps haunting her.

Sadly they have to leave and return home and she, try as she may, has not been able to reach the little boy. She's extremely disappointed by this. They arrive home and unpack and later the husband drops off their film for processing.

A few days later they're sitting on the couch, going through their pictures and reliving some of the fun moments, when they both stop dead in their tracks. She is holding a picture in her hands of her and her husband asleep in the hotel bed in the middle of the night, taken from the vantage point of the dresser where she would always leave her camera.

So, who took the picture?

They believe it was the little boy's way of asking "how do you like it when someone tries to take a picture of you when you don't want them to?"

Um, yeah, again… no thank you!

ANECDOTE: THE CHILD ON THE TOUR - *Sidney Smith*

Many years ago, I was leading a Haunted History ghost tour throughout the French Quarter. Our tours are primarily geared toward an adult audience. Not that there's anything inappropriate for kids, it's just that the material is more easily digested by a more mature audience. This particular group included a single mother and her son who looked to be about 6 or 7 years old. He was the ONLY child on the tour.

About 30 minutes in to the tour, the child started walking along side of me, as kids are often drawn to the tour guide with questions. I could easily see the mother toward the back of the group the entire time. About 30 minutes into that, the mom comes running up to me frantically screaming, "Have you seen my child???" I pointed downward at the kid who was standing right next to me the whole time. After a sigh of relief, she then stated, "WOW! He was with me just a second ago." And I'm thinking to myself, NO...He's been with me for the last 30 minutes.

She then looked down at the child and in a frustrated tone asked him, "Why did you leave me???" He innocently looked up at her and said..."Because you were holding that other boy's hand, mommy."

Ghost kids in Williamsburg VA –
Photo by Dionysios Evangelopoulos

THE KIDS IN THE PARK
Charmaine Swan Rich

This chapter is about my job and all the people I come in contact with, the ones that are alive...and dead. I am a tour guide in New Orleans. In doing this job, I found my "gift" or "curse". People call it different things – depending their perspective.

I always knew I was able to hear, see, and feel the spirits, but never really talked about it. I guess those few naysayers invaded my confidence. This job has taught me that, and so have the spirits. I started working as a tour guide 2 years ago and one of the main tours I give is our bus tour. We escort groups all around the city to haunted locations and regale them about the history of the city. It truly is a wonderful, fun job. I have a great time with the tourists, being a people person, but I have also reestablished my connection with the spirit world.

I always knew it was there, ever since I was a little girl. Our stiff concrete society dictates I don't talk about that. But the spirits kept coming, little by little... and this job and one of my wonderful bosses, who has become my mentor, helped me understand my connection with the spirits. Let me clarify my boss calls me an empath, a spirit magnet. They have been coming to visit me all my life. Some time ago, I finally fully accepted it. I am not a psychic or medium and will never claim to be. The spirits just visit me. At times I can see them, hear them, feel them – but the level and amount of contact is up to them. At first, yes, I was scared, and felt like I was crazy, but now, you get used to things happening, sometimes they just startle me. This leads me to my City Park story.

On our bus tour, one stop is in City Park. It was founded as a park in 1854 by John McDonough who bought the land from a man named Louis Allard. The park was formally known as the Allard Plantation. So, as you can guess – there are lots of spirits who inhabit the park. The tour bus always stops by an exceptionally large live oak tree (about 300-400 years old) next a lagoon. It is the perfect place for spirits to roam and, it is my favorite location on the tour. A live oak growing next to water is the best ingredients for a portal for the spirits. Especially in New Orleans. We honor our dead and talk to them, call them for advice, for support and thank them for our many blessings. We also love to raise the vibration in New Orleans. We do this through music and food, as well as by celebrating and being together, being a family. We are all connected through our energy with one another and this energy connects us to our ancestors. But, the main reason why this is my favorite location is that my "kids" are there, always waiting for me.

The tour originally went to this location to tell our guests a story about Lisa. Since she is a highly active spirit, this location is very popular with the tourists and they can take lots of pictures of her. Her story dates back to when City Park was the Allard Plantation. Legend tells us that since Lisa drowned herself in the lagoon, and sometimes she still makes her appearance there. We encountered other spirits there – lots of them – and it happened by accident.

Child Spirits visit with Charmaine Swan Rich during her story at City Park – Photo by Charmaine Swan Rich

One night my boss was giving this particular tour and her friend who was tagging along, just happened to be a psychic medium. Upon arriving at the lagoon, the medium begins to walk away from the group. Naturally, my boss realized he discovered someone. And, she was right. That was the first time the kids made an appearance. That night, the medium found 9 children there – who had been brought to this location, killed there and either buried or thrown into the lagoon. We suspect that we are the first to find them.

Child Ghost in a Dress, City Park, 2019
– Photo by Charmaine Swan Rich

Then, later tour groups began taking pictures of a little boy at this location. He showed up a lot. We had to find out who he was, who the kids were, and what had happened here. My boss then scheduled a ghost hunt at this location. She brought in another medium (who had no idea what the first medium found out) who brought out equipment. I went on this hunt and was the one filming the psychic. Which, by the way, is easier said than done. I will never forget that night – we did find out who the little boy was…and more.

That night our psychic connected with the little boy in the pictures and we found out his story. This little boy's name is George. George is there with 3 other little girls. The four kids stick together. George told us they are all about 9-12 years old and died in the 1920s. George told us a serial killer killed them. Since he always carried around a bag of toys, he would give them a toy and whistle a fun tune to get them away from their parents, either at home or from the amusement park just down the street. He would walk them to the large oak tree by the lagoon.

This is where he would kill them and bury them. That night George told our psychic he is here playing with his yo-yo and waiting for his older brother. We asked George if this was the toy the killer gave him. He said it was. We then asked him how he died? How did the kids die? George told us the killer crushed their skulls.

George also talked about how the killer used to whistle and so he thought this man was a hobo. He traveled from city to city – by jumping on trains. We did some research and found that the large street at this location, called City Park Ave, was a railroad line.

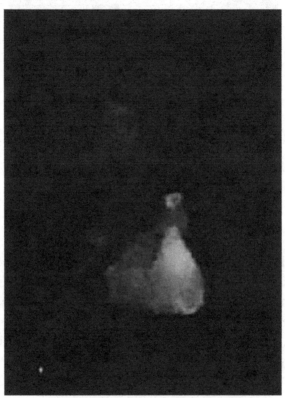

Ghost with a Bag, City Park, 2019
– Photo by Charmaine Swan Rich

That night George also told the psychic that the kids now love to watch people in the park, their favorite thing to do. There is a beautiful pavilion across the lagoon where City Park hosts large events, like fundraisers or weddings. When there is an event there – the kids will sit at the water's edge and watch the people dance and listen to the music. They love to do this.

I wondered why the kids are still here. I read and researched to find out that some earth- bound spirits stay with us because they have unfinished business. The more I go to this location, the more I realize the kids want us to know that they are there. They want people to know their story. Since we did this hunt, George and the girls have constantly made themselves known. Just about every tour I conduct, the group leaves with pictures of the spirits. Spirits show themselves in many different ways. Also, as we bring more and more groups there – the spirits get more and more energy to manifest.

The more I did this tour, the more George connected with me. A common question which tourists ask me now is, "don't you get scared?" The answer, "Yes-at first." But when you are around the same location and, probably the same spirits, night after night, you know which ones are scary and which ones really need company. Do not get me wrong, there is also an evil spirit at this location, sometimes, but I will talk about him later.

Every time I got off the bus, I could feel and hear George saying – "she's here again!" They respond to the excitement that I came to visit and brought some company for them. There were some nights when George and the girls were so excited they would, for lack of a better way to say, clog up my brain. I would hear their thoughts, their excitement, and it was so overwhelming I couldn't speak, I couldn't give the tour. I didn't know these people on the tour, but they expected me to tell a story. There were times, when I had to excuse myself for a minute and let the kids know I would give them attention AFTER I told their story. You know how kids are – very impatient. As I did this and would turn back to my group, I saw looks of fear, amazement, and skepticism on their faces. Some people, actually most people, were amazed and wanted to know what the kids were telling me and how I could feel them and hear them. But there were the few who thought I was nuts and "acting" – those doubters always gave bad reviews. I have now learned to ignore them and feel a bit sorry for them.

I not only hear George in my head, but I sometimes see him and the girls. Early on, George told me he would really like it if the people sang to him and the girls. They loved music. I would tell my groups this, and those that sang – did get wonderful pictures of orbs, mist etc. George really didn't care what they sang or how they sounded. He would always connect with people that either sang to him or talked to him – sincere people. George and the girls would usually pull me to one area or another. I would tell the people on my tour to "take a picture over there." Most of the time they would go home with a wonderful picture of a spirit.

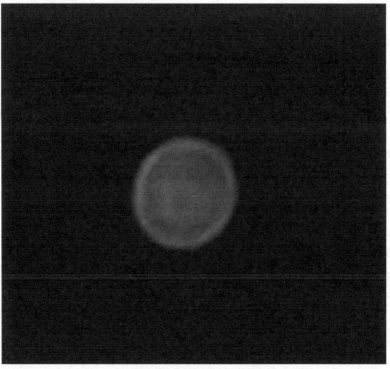

George Visiting the Tour, City Park, 2019
– Photo by Charmaine Swan Rich

I have had lots of experiences with the kids. One night, the kids just couldn't wait until I got off the bus. As we pulled up to the location, the driver looked at the bus door and told me not to move. I stood still as he took a picture of the door. He was a bit shaken. I asked him what he saw. He said, "I'll tell you later." Now, for all of our tours, the driver stays on the bus, and does not know the story about the kids. The tour continued and the next stop was the bathroom break. At this point I asked the driver what he saw. He said, "I saw kids standing by the glass door, gazing into the bus."

I told him those are the spirits that are always here, as it was 10:30pm and there were no kids anywhere that night. The bus driver became confused and said, "Well, the picture didn't come out because of the flash, but these kids looked evil!" I reassured him the kids were not evil and asked him why he thought this. He answered, "There was something wrong with their heads, they were misshaped, crushed." I then told him how the kids died. He got very pale. Now this driver never gets off the bus on our tours!

As I mentioned before, there are many spirits at this location. There is at least one evil, scary spirit that we know about. It is the serial killer, at least we think it is. There have been times I have gotten off the bus and felt something was horribly wrong, a dreading feeling, like I should not be there. These are the times you need to leave – trust your instincts when it comes to the spirit world. But, in this case, the show must go on. I would take my groups out and tell them the story.

During these times, I have learned not to stay long at this location. One night, during a feeling of dread, a couple of teens asked me specific information about the serial killer. I do make it a point to not talk about him as much as possible. He is part of the story, but, that's it. Well, this one night, I didn't listen to my instincts, I wanted the tips, and admittedly, I got cocky.

Right by the oak tree I went into details about the serial killer as much as we knew. The tourists were hanging on my every word, and the dread was spreading. We got back on the dark bus and I felt something crawling on my neck, right by my vocal cords. Mind you, this is 11pm at night. I instinctively crushed the thing and to this day, I have no idea what it was. I threw it on the floor of the bus and felt my neck. There was a stinger about ½ inch long in my neck. Panic hit me in front of my tour group. This is not good. I pulled the stinger out and tried to continue with the tour. No one really knew what was going on, as the bus was very dark. And, thank God the next stop was our bathroom break. Everyone always runs off the bus to the bathrooms.

I then looked in the mirror on the bus, lights on, to see a hole in my neck, and it was swelling up the size of a lemon! It was right in my vocal cords and I could not speak! The bus started to spin, and I had to sit down with help from the bus driver. As he ran to get me water, I took Benadryl from my purse. A good tour guide always carries a knife, ibuprofen, Benadryl, and bug spray, which may have helped in this situation. I took the Benadryl – actually two – with my water.

As I sat and tried to calm myself down, I realized what I had done. Never, never talk about him. He is evil. I paid the price, the serial killer had sent me a message right where it hurt me as a guide, in my vocal cords. I got the message. I have never talked about him while standing in the location. Luckily, I was able to continue and thanks to the Benadryl, I was quite happy and mellow the rest of the tour.

The last time I saw George was early March 2020…one of the last times I did the bus tour thanks to the COVID-19 virus. I was telling my group the story of the kids and I looked to my right by an azalea bush. George was standing there, smiling at me. I gasped and froze for about 5 seconds – which seemed an eternity when you have 28 people starring at you. Of course, no one else saw him and I didn't reveal what I saw. I then just continued with the story. I know George wanted me to come to the azalea bush. When I finished, a couple of girls did ask me why I gasped. I told them. They were amazed and happy that George was there. I did walk over to the azalea bush – which had just started blooming pretty white flowers. I could hear George telling me that he wanted to show me the pretty flowers.

It has been about 8 weeks since I did this tour and I miss the kids terribly. Later I did go back to the tree during the day for a walk. I brought my kitty, Minnie. She is an exceedingly rare black kitty who loves to walk on a leash. I walked her to the tree that day to meet George. I explained to him that day why we were not doing tours and that one day, when the virus goes away, we will do the tours again. I hoped he understood, as much as a kid can. So, I guess this virus has even affected the spirits – they really are not seeing many people in the park. Thus, not getting the energy they need to materialize.

I always have tourists ask me, "Does anything ever follow you home?" I always find this question odd – anything? It should be anyone. And that answer is yes. I think the kids come home with me sometimes. But, not for long, and I do not know why. My good friend, who is also an empath has told me she believes the kids know that I am a mom and feels that motherly bond with me. And, that's OK with me. I love being a mom. It really is who I am in my soul.

Twice when I was home alone, I heard a male, child voice saying "Mom!" At other times things have been moved around in the kitchen and sounds coming from the kitchen when no one is there. There have been two occasions when my husband has come to me yelling, "Someone is here!!!! There is something going on in the kitchen!!" All I do is smile and laugh when he leaves the room. I do believe it is the kids making him a little nuts – as kids do.

Finally, I will leave you with a thought – the spirits are all around us, every day, every night. Trying to communicate. We just must know how to listen, what to look for. The very last bus tour I did before the COVID 19 virus outbreak was a private tour. Lots of drunk people, so lots of energy. And, a good percentage of naysayers. Sometimes my favorite tour. We went to the live oak tree at City Park and right away I could tell the kids really did not want to come out for drunk adults. So, I thought, well, they may only see spirits because of the spirits they are drinking. Ha! Once again, the spirits world proved me wrong. That was the tour they were trying to send a message – a dark one, one no one wants. I realized this after our sobering lockdown for the COVID 19 virus.

This last picture, of the dark, menacing soul, is the very last picture taken on my bus tour before COVID 19 came to New Orleans. I did not realize this was a sign until I was sitting in my house, day after day, becoming a bit dark myself.
So, if one day, you find yourself wanting to take a vacation, after all this COVID 19 virus leaves us, come on down to New Orleans. George and the kids are waiting for you, and maybe, someone else.... I would love to introduce you to them.....

A Lady in Black at City Park – Selfie Takers to the right are unaware of her presence. This figure appeared on Charmaine's last tour before the Covid 19 shutdown. (Both photos courtesy of Charmaine Swan Rich)

ANECDOTE: THE PUB CRAWL OF THE TRAVELING PANTS

My early Sunday evening Pub Crawl started normal enough, semi drunk bachelor party, about a dozen nice young guys having fun, nothing out of the ordinary. I'm standing just off the curb, as we guides always do, telling them about our first in ground cemetery at Burgundy and St. Peter, when a car comes up really close behind me and stops. The window rolls down and a gentleman about my age is driving. He turns and grabs something off of the passenger seat and moves to stick it out the window, just as a member of my tour group steps off the sidewalk behind me and approaches the vehicle. The guy in the car hands him what appears to be a pair of tuxedo pants on a hanger, and that was, in fact, exactly what it was. This kid on my tour had left his tux pants at home and was supposed to be in the wedding the next day with the guys on my tour. His dad drove out from Biloxi to drop them off and tracked him down right to the corner on which we stood. Well done good sir, you didn't even have to exit the car. The kid finished the rest of the Pub Crawl carrying those pants around on a hanger. He never dropped his pants and he never spilled a drop. Not all heroes wear capes!

7

THE WATCHER ON THE ROOF TOP
727 Toulouse Street

Vampires play a significant part of New Orleans folklore, dating back to the late 1720's, where it is said that they made the trek from the old world (Europe) to the new world hidden securely in the dowry boxes of the Casket Girls. Jacques St. Germaine, a prominent figure in New Orleans society in the early 1900's also plays heavily into this vampire lore and was reportedly a character influence in Anne Rice's Interview with a Vampire.

So one evening I'm standing with my tour group across the street from Molly's Bar discussing Comte St. Germaine when I glance back toward the bar and I see, what I can only describe as a dark figure hunched on the rooftop by the chimney, watching us. Then suddenly, it stands up, unfurls, and disappears in an instant. It happened so fast that I, as they old saying goes "didn't believe my own eyes."

I remember pausing for a moment as my brain registered the event and turned to my group to ask if anyone else had witnessed what I had just seen. That's when I saw a lady in my group standing with her mouth agape, eyes wide and completely motionless. I asked her if she just saw something on the roof. She said yes. I asked her to describe it to me, and she did. Exactly as I had seen it occur. A few others in my group also attested to seeing a "blur of motion" on the rooftop, but not in the detail in which the lady on my tour and I had witnessed.

The Dark Rooftop on Toulouse

My wife and I were living on Frenchmen street at the time and I remember walking home after the tour, a little unnerved and paying special attention to the rooftops. I posted on Facebook that evening about my encounter and Kalila Smith, a New Orleans paranormal expert, friend, and mentor, weighed in.

She stated that this is a frequent occurrence, though rarely observed, and believes that they are watching to see if we treat their stories with respect. Recent documented encounters have occurred at Maison De Ville (where we were standing), Jackson Square and The French Market Inn.

The Jackson Square incident was documented, as it was reported to police in 2013. Three young ladies, walking through Jackson Square around midnight one evening, noticed a man standing on the roof of St. Louis Cathedral watching them as they passed on the walk way below. He leaned out further and they immediately "felt threatened". One of the girls screamed and the figure was suddenly "gone in a flash".

Many locals believe this to have been an encounter with Jacques St. Germaine, or as he is known now, Vampire Jack. His impending arrival is usually heralded by an intermediary who will approach the intended victim on the street or sidewalk and utter the phrase "It's a nice night for Jack to be out." Most people brush off these odd encounters with a "good for him" type response and then go on about their business. That is, until they meet a strange dark figure further along their path and come to the realization that they are missing time, and also have strange cut, or wound, on their bodies which they can't recall how they received.

Since my little tour encounter I always endeavor to keep my stories respectful and walk with one eye on the rooftops. You never know. In a city like New Orleans, perhaps this is not just folklore after all.

Vampires on my Tour!

Amanda the Vampire Hunter

Author's Note: If you're interested, Kalila Smith relates similar stories in her book New Orleans Ghosts, Voodoo and Vampires, Journey into Darkness, which is a must have book regarding the paranormal in New Orleans, in my opinion.

ANECDOTE: QUEEN FOR A DAY

In 1981 Queen came to New Orleans to rehearse prior to launching their South American tour. They posed for an iconic picture on the corner of Royal and Toulouse (Goggle: Queen New Orleans) which we stop and recreate on my Haunted History Pub Crawl Tour.

Note the very important role, that one guy has taken (bottom left), that I have dubbed "Nose picking guy". Check out the back left of original Queen photo online and you'll see what I mean.

GHOST RENTALS

Whenever I give a Haunted Pub Crawl tour I feel the responsibility to act as a good host for my tour patrons. During the decade my wife and I were visiting as tourists we were always fortunate to get friendly and engaging tour guides that treated us well. It made for a more fulfilling experience.

Now that I'm in that position I make an effort to get to know the people on my tour, converse with them about their stay and offer my assistance whenever possible, because I sincerely care that they also have a good experience. It's just part of being an ambassador for the city. This means that while people are watching me give a tour I'm also watching them and looking for non-verbal cues and body language to gauge their reactions, good and bad.

One Sunday evening in May of 2018 one such experience really stood out and left an impression on me. I had the usual full twenty eight person tour group on a Sunday evening and I noticed during my first story that these two young couples, who were standing together, were extremely quiet and disengaged. Almost to the point of deep sadness, like they had just received some really bad news.

At our first bar stop I made a point of introducing myself, asking where they were from (Southern California) and if there was any special occasion they were celebrating on their visit to New Orleans. They were polite enough during the conversation, but still seemed down, so I asked them if there was anything wrong. They all dropped their heads in unison and told me that they'd had a pretty horrifying experience on their way home from partying Saturday night and it had nothing to do with the paranormal.

They told me they had a really fun night partying in the French Quarter, where they stayed until about 2am. Because it was a beautiful spring evening they decided to walk back to their Airbnb instead of getting a cab or an Uber. It was only about a mile outside of the Quarter. They were talking and laughing and the girls decided to race each other for fun, and soon left the guys walking back about half a block behind. As they girls got close to a neighborhood bank they slowed and resumed walking, still a good distance from the guys, lagging behind.

That's when a man exited the passenger side of a parked car, leveled an AK-47 at them and demanded their purses. The two girls screamed and started to run. Their two husbands, hearing the screams started running and yelling in their direction. Apparently it startled the perpetrator enough that he decided to jump back in the car and they made a fast get away before the husbands caught up with them. They were all understandably terrified and traumatized.

They got to the Airbnb and spent time, into the wee hours of the morning, going over the incident with the police. At one point they started packing their things and were just going to cut their losses, end their trip, and get as far away from the city as possible. But as they started to relax a bit, and the adrenalin wore off, fatigue set in and they to get some sleep. They ended up sleeping most of the day and decided go ahead and keep their reservation on their ghost tour. My tour.

Honestly, I was speechless. And heartbroken for them. I remember telling them, over and over, how sorry I was. They accepted it graciously and we continued on the tour. I kept tabs on them at each stop and noticed, with each gruesome and haunting tale, that they began to relax and enjoy themselves and that their spirits were lifting. At the end of the tour they came up and hugged me and thanked me for "saving" their trip. They said the experience was just what they needed to give the city another chance. We took pictures together (which I won't post since I don't have their contact info to obtain permission) and had a few drinks together. I gave them my number, but failed to get theirs, which I regret, because the AK-47 robber was eventually arrested a few weeks later and jailed. I would have liked to have let them know.

That encounter, to this day, is still one of my proudest moments as a guide in this city that I love and call home. It also deeply saddened and angered me. Angered me because in that particular neighborhood where the incident occurred, well, it hasn't actually been fair to call it a neighborhood for quite some time. Since Katrina it has turned into blocks and blocks of empty corporate Airbnb investment properties. This lack of community infrastructure also makes these areas a haven for criminals as ill-informed tourists, unaware of the circumstances, are ripe to become victims.

Fortunately, in the summer of 2019, the City woke up and realized that whole historic communities were being decimated by this practice, and families, some who had spent generations in some of these houses, were forced out because they could no longer afford the artificially increased property taxes.

So the city did the right thing for these neighborhoods and ended the whole house rental practice. At the time of this writing property values are starting to return to somewhat affordable levels again, and hopefully we'll soon see families back populating these ghost communities, many which surround the periphery of the Quarter, once again.

I also make it a point to end my tours by reminding my guests that this city has a dark side and can be very dangerous, so to be careful, act with caution, don't get so drunk that you become unaware of your surroundings and get transport home if it's outside the Quarter. Especially late at night. We all want you to be safe, fall in love with the city the same way we did, and come back and visit us over and over again. It's what truly makes this all worthwhile.

A few month after launching the Haunted Pub Crawl in early 2017, things were blowing up and the Crawl was becoming quite popular. Sidney threw some of his best guides, Drew Cothern, Randy Walker and Chrissie McArdle on the tour, and working together we were putting together a really solid tour experience with great bar stops.

Soon after, that's when I learned that espionage wasn't just limited to my Defense Department experience. One Monday evening I had a fair sized group, maybe about ten people, on my early tour. We launched right at 5:30, got drinks and I started in on my first story. A tale of the most devastating fire in New Orleans history, and a few of the victims who still occupied the building in which we stood.

About half way through the story, two young ladies walked in to the room where we were gathered and demanded to know why we didn't wait for them. Taken aback for a moment, I welcomed them, told them they hadn't really missed anything and that I would catch them up on what they had missed between stops. That didn't satisfy them and I could see the rest of the group was getting impatient with the interruption, so I asked them to have a seat and we would talk at the conclusion of the story.

They sat with their arms folded, like petulant little kids, and glared at me until I finished. That's when I laid it out for them. They were 15 minutes late. Out of respect for our clients, we start on time. If someone is late they have two options; realize that they're now on the tour, albeit late, relax and continue with the group, or, go ask for a refund. That's it.

Unfortunately they decided to continue on, which I later discovered, was by design. They refused to buy drinks at the stops, not spending any money, which is a tell-tale sign, and asked bizarre and pointedly skeptical questions at the end of each story. Something didn't feel right, so I pressed them a few times for details about themselves in the form of casual chit chat. They always responded with vague and sometimes contradictory answers. They were definitely up to something. I snuck a picture of them at one point and after my tour, reported the incident to my management. Something was off.

A few days later I got my answer. They were guides from a rival tour company sent to undermine my tour and find out what stories we were telling and why we were becoming so popular. They even posted a bogus negative review mentioning that their company did a much better job of this tour and review readers should come and take it from them instead. Pretty cut throat and low class. Fortunately our management was on top of that and had the bogus review removed.

This is why I always recommend that people read several reviews prior to going to a restaurant, taking a tour, checking out a band, etc. Sometimes people have nefarious motives in their reviews, they have a vendetta, they got their feelings hurt somehow, or, in this instance, they're trying to steal customers. Reviewer beware. It's a jungle out there.

**Things are getting pretty cut throat on St. Peter Street
with Claire Christine Sargenti - 2018**

9

THE LALAURIE MANSION
1140 Royal Street

I'm sure many of you are already familiar with the story of the LaLaurie Mansion, from either taking one of our tours or perhaps from watching American Horror Story, Season Three, Coven. I can't think of anyone better than incomparable Kathie Bates to portray Delphine Marie McCarty LaLaurie, a 1800s New Orleans socialite who is considered to be amongst America's first female serial killers. Most notably for torturing and murdering her enslaved people, sometimes even during her lavish dinner parties.

In July 2016 I had only been a tour guide for a few months when I got the assignment for my first private tour. I was to meet my point of contact outside of Muriel's restaurant at 8pm, right outside Jackson Square. I showed up a little early, texted my contact that I was waiting outside and then, promptly at 8pm, eighteen bachelorettes, with Bride Tribe tank tops and glowing penises on their heads, marched out of the restaurant and lined up in from of me. I... was terrified. Not because of who they were, but rather, because of who I was. I mean, here's an old retired dude pushing sixty taking out a group of young girls on a private tour.

I was afraid that they would have wanted a younger guide, somebody they could party with and relate to. I learned a valuable lesson that night. Never judge how you think the tour is going to go based on how the crowd looks when you walk up, because, you know what? These girls were awesome. They were fun, accepting and totally embraced the tour and me as their guide. Oh yeah, they were also terrified. Of everything. Which makes my job a whole lot easier and a lot more fun. I pulled out all the stops that I could muster with my whole three months of tour guide experience and, towards the end, when they asked if could go to the LaLaurie Mansion so that they could take pictures. How could I say no?

I led them there, told them the story, in gruesome detail, and then motioned for them to follow me across the street so they could look at the property and maybe even get a peek in the windows. I got half way across the street and realized I was by myself. I turned to look and they were all still standing firm where I left them. Not one of them had budged. I yelled back "come on guys!" and they yelled back "NO WAY!" And I said, "Seriously, no one is home" and they responded "Not the living people we're worried about." I shrugged it off, fair enough, and rejoined the group while they finished taking pictures from the safety of across the street. We said our goodbyes and I went home feeling pretty good about myself at that point and hoped they would leave me a good review.

Two AM. My phone starts blowing up. "OMG, OMG, do you see what is in this picture!!!???" So I sat up in bed, looked, and was pretty much blown away. Check it out for yourself.

The LaLaurie Mansion – Original Photo - Circled

Bachelorette Party Photo - Zoom

There is a superstition amongst some of the guides and investigators that walking in a cavalier fashion under the gallery at the LaLaurie Mansion will result in a curse. Now, as a rule I don't particularly subscribe to those types of things, but this one certainly gave me pause. Remember, this is New Orleans and the rules, they don't much apply down here. And this lady in black, grey face and dark hooded cloak, staring back at the girl taking the picture, to me, that's a big fat nope.

Now, before you think maybe I'm not as skeptical as I should be on some of these things, I did take the following steps to verify the authenticity of this photo. First, I spoke with the girl who took it the next morning. She claimed that they were sitting in Laffite's Blacksmith Shop after my tour having drinks and going through their pictures. As soon as she saw the picture in question, and zoomed in to look at the apparition, her phone died in her hand, in spite having more than half a battery life left on her phone. It freaked her TF out.

Once she could get back to their hotel and recharge her phone, she did. It took over an hour. Super drained. And once it came back, that's when she started blowing up my phone at two AM. When I spoke with her she said she hadn't slept much that night.

Next thing I did was drive to the location the next morning to see if I had somehow missed something in the window. Did somebody leave a rain coat hanging in the window? Nope. Nothing there. Now I had checked the alarm system, which is visible, through the side window of the entry door when we were there the night before. That's why I was confident during our visit that no one was home. I checked it again and, still set. No one home.

Next step was to send the picture to a forensic IT specialist friend of mine that works in DOD. The verdict; authentic. No evidence of manipulation whatsoever. Final step, send it to a paranormal investigator for validation and comments. What I got back was a little lesson in Paranormal Investigation 101.

So, why do investigators on shows like Ghost Hunters and Kindred Spirits (one of my personal favorites) go dark during their investigations? Is it for mood? To make it look more scary? No. It's because we believe spirits need to draw on energy in order to manifest and interact with the physical plane of existence. That's why investigators put out those boxes that light up, or go beep, pumping out a lot of energy so spirits can draw from that energy and communicate.

From my experience there is probably no greater power source on the planet than a bachelorette party visiting New Orleans and this spirit came out to warn them, not in my house girls.

Terrified Guests outside the LaLaurie Mansion

Okay bachelorettes, who's next?

"THE SPACES IN BETWEEN"

Oh yeah, in my time in between tours I also get to play music!

With Ro Lopez, Halloween 2017

Halloween 2016

With Wild Card – Alice Cooper in Wonderland – 2018
With Claire Voorhies-Chighizola, Chris Primm & Jim Mitchell

Halloween 2018 with Wild Card

The Away Team with Ro Lopez, Chris Primm & Jim Mitchell – 2017

Dark Amber at Santos – August 2019 with Joey Laborde on Bass

Olas Ortwein, Kyle Cripps & Amber Mouton – Quarter Life 2019

AND WE LOVE TO COSTUME… FOR EVERYTHING!

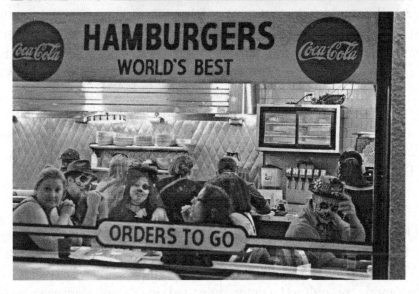

10

NIGHTS SPENT IN THE GUTTER WITH THE RATS AND THE PUNKS
Drew Cothern

The French Quarter is famously a place of personalities. Ruthie the Duck Girl, who wore brightly colored furs and roller skated the old Creole streets accompanied by a small flock the birds in the latter days of the Twentieth Century; the Traffic Tranny, who up until recently would help motorists safely pass through the throngs of revelers on Bourbon Street at St. Ann; Twerkin' Granny, who can still be found delivering her message of God's love as she pedals through the neighborhood on her improvised bike/billboard/party-wagon, stopping every now and then to dance with her fans in groovy, geriatric gyrations. These eccentrics add the color, vivacity, and unpredictability that makes the Quarter famous around the world, and they are beloved while they're here and mourned when they're not.

Then there are the gutterpunks.

Oogles. Crust-punks. Traveling Kids. Neo-Hobos. There are plenty of terms for them, but in New Orleans, we call them gutterpunks. You've no doubt seen them in your city, in whatever passes for an economic or cultural center, crowded in vacant doorways and alcoves and cluttering up corners, uniformed in earth tones and face tattoos and body odor and contempt, all alike in their desperate attempts to be different, often with dogs in tow.

Some of them had hard home lives that they had escaped, perhaps too young to be out on the streets and hopping trains alone. Some of them had dependencies on drug or drink that dragged them down and put them out. Some seem to be doing it for a lark, retaining a credit card or a trust-fund for their endeavors. Some have a philosophy built on anarchism, Beat generation romance for a life *On the Road*, and the DIY sensibilities of punks that had come before. They can be crude, obnoxious, and mean, but on a personal level, I find that I can often get along with them well enough when I'm not working. I've always sympathized with the outsider. When I'm trying to guide a tour, it's another story.

Gutterpunks are the enemy of French Quarter tour guides.

I understand the impulse. When you're on the fringe of society, why not shake things up, provide some much needed distraction from your hunger, your withdrawals, or even just your boredom? You come upon some jerky-looking asshole dressed in a bowler hat and red-checkered vest, carrying a cane, telling tired old bullshit ghost stories to a bunch of square tourists, and friend, you've got your distraction.

Looking back over the years at the way I used to dress in an attempt to add a touch of theatricality to my presentation, I'd have bullied me too. But I quickly learned that the only thing it really adds is a signal to the gutterpunks that you're still green, still unsure, and totally ready to be fucked with. At five years in, I don't dress like that anymore, and the gutterpunks tend to recognize me as one who has been taken in and accepted by the Quarter, no longer shakable, and ultimately not worth the trouble. But that was not always the case.

Photo by Drew Cothern

I recorded the first interaction I had with a gutterpunk while on tour. He was drunk, I was working. I was dressed in the outfit I wore my first season, a bowler hat, red checkered vest, and black pants. I also carried my grandfather's cane. This is the exchange that followed, documented shortly after it occurred:

"Thass all bullshit."

"Excuse me? Which part?"

"Alla it."

"Oh, my mistake. Ladies and gentlemen, I didn't realize we had a true historian in our midst. Would you like to lead the tour?"

"Put down your stick, dude."

"No, I need it. Gummy leg. Besides, I'm sure you'll do fine without it. Go ahead. Tell these fine people what you know about New Orleans history."

"Do y'all know about the House of the Risin' Sun?"

"I do, actually, yes. But go on."

"Well...iss been the ruin of many poor boys..."

"Uh-huh. Go on."

"Put your stick down."

"Why?"

"Because I'm gonna fight you."

"Oh. In that case, no way. Why do you wanna fight me?"

"Because you tol' me to lead yer tour."

"Oh, I'm sorry! I got the impression you knew what you were talking about. But you DON'T know what you're talking about, do you?"

"It was my birfday yesterday. Somebody stabbed me in the foot and I'm PISSED OFF about it!"

"Well, I'm sure it was just karma paying a debt."

"PUT YOUR STICK DOWN!"

"LOOK! This is gonna go one of two ways - you're either going to mosey on your way, or I'mma get NOPD down here. Which's it gonna be?"

"Aww, man, I just wanted to fight, dude. You ain't gotta call the cops, man, you ain't gotta call the cops."

"Phone's ringing."

"You're skinny and quick and I'm slow. You ain't gotta call the cops, dude, you prolly coulda taken me. Pussy."

He hung his head as he hobbled away, careful not to put any weight on his stabbed foot. My group applauded. For a brief moment, I pitied him. A *very* brief moment. So, this is the way these interactions typically go. Words, threats, insults, but nothing more. On a couple of memorable occasions, though, that was not the case.

I'll never forget this one, because the fellow was wearing a white t-shirt displaying the Ten of Swords from the tarot as seen in the Rider-Waite deck, with a figure evoking an assassinated Julius Caesar lying on the ground in a pool of blood, run through with ten swords. It represents betrayal, loss, defeat, failure, and death; in other words, not necessarily something one would normally wish to have hanging over them. It was a card he seemed to be living.

I had an unusually courteous group that night. Normally, I have to keep reminding them to leave a walking path behind them so as not to block traffic on the sidewalk, but not this time. In spite of this,

Ten of Swords came sauntering by and seemed to have a problem that there were people gathered on the sidewalk. He said something snide to one of my guests, who responded in kind. I was going to ignore it, but it kept going and the gutterpunk was getting more aggressive. So I stopped my story and said, "Is there a problem?"

The gutterpunk said, "Yeah, all these fuggin white people are blocking up the sidewalk! It's giving me anxiety- white people give me anxiety!" Now, it's worth noting that this fellow was white, whiter than my group, even, which was maybe a quarter Hispanic.

Confused by his statement, I said, "White people give you anxiety? Man, looking in the mirror must be tough for you." Then, after noting his scruffy state, "Although I guess you haven't done that in a while."

He turned on me, "FUCK YOU! Eat your Chick-Fil-A!"

"What?"

"Eat flesh, breathe chemicals, GET FUCKED!"

I cocked my head and looked at him. "You're cute. You're really very cute. With your half-baked philosophies, your sense of entitlement, and your hate. Just adorable!"

"I'll show you fucking CUTE!" he roared, throwing down his skateboard and box of take-out to rush me.

As I have learned to do in these situations, I did not flinch. I did not back down. And all of a sudden, he lost the courage of his convictions. He glared at me for a moment before casting his eyes down to his spilled take-out.

"That was my fucking DINNER!" he moaned.

"Then why'd you throw it on the ground?"

He knelt down and grabbed a fistful of runny noodles off the dirty St. Phillips Street sidewalk, and took a bite out of it. It was only then that true disgust washed over me. He glared at me, then hurled his fistful of noodles at me. His aim was bad. Very bad. The noodles flew over my head without even having to duck, landing in the street behind me with a wet splat. I laughed. My group laughed. And with a final fuck-you, he stalked off into the night, leaving the rest of his dinner behind. Other tour guides would see him following our altercation getting into a fight with a parked car on Bourbon. I would see Ten of Swords only once more, a few weeks later, being thrown out of the St. Louis Cathedral. His shirt, which had been white when he assaulted me with Alfredo, was torn and brown. I wouldn't see him again.

Photo by Drew Cothern

Perhaps the most memorable interaction I've had, though, came while I was telling a story in Dutch Alley by the River. I was near the end of my tour with a group that, frankly, didn't care for me. They were disengaged, dead-eyed, like goldfish in a bowl, gawping at me as I talked, but not really hearing. I hate groups like that. May as well be telling ghost stories to a brick wall.

Enter: a gutterpunk. He comes oiling by, passing in between me and my group. It seems that he's just passing through, but then he stops. He stops right in front of a girl that looks like she just graduated high school in Cornfuck, Nebraska. He eyes her before holding up his grubby hand, bringing it right up to her face. She reacts the way you might expect any valedictorian of Cornfuck High might - she gasps and cringes away.

I sighed. I approached him and said, "Hey, man. You gotta go. I'm working here, and you're bothering these people."

"I ain't goin' nowhere until I get my high-five," he snarled, turning back to the girl.

"Yes, you are," I said, feeling uncharacteristically heroic, "One way or another."

He wheeled around on me, got right in my face, smashing his nose into mine. "You gonna head-butt me?" he said.

I gripped my cane, ready to smash him in the temple as soon as he made a move. My adrenaline began pumping hard. I was wearing steel-toe boots and ready to stomp him right into the ground if necessary. I had plenty of witnesses who would say I was justified. Just as soon as he made the first move. I waited. He waited. We were breathing each other's air. I'd put him in a bad position, I realized. If I hit him first, then he was justified in giving me a beating. But if he just walked away, then I would win. So he settled on the third option, to attempt to humiliate me. So he kissed me, full on. Open-mouth.

But here's the thing. I'm not about to be humiliated by some goddamn gutterpunk.

I kissed him back with tongue.

A power-move! He pulled back, his eyes wide with surprise. I wiped my mouth and fixed him with my most intimidating gaze and growled, *"Yeah!"*

In that growl, I had asserted, *Yeah, that's right. Fuck with me. I can be crazy. I can live in the ditch with you. Yeah. Fuck with me. I dare you.* But he didn't. We'd met as shameless equals. There was nothing more to be said. Then, he was gone, down the road to the river. As he went, I realized I could taste his rancid sweat on my mustache. I grimaced and spit before turning to my group.

"Y'ALL BETTER TIP ME FOR THAT!" I bellowed.

For the first time all night, these dead-eyed fish-people that I couldn't get to even chuckle began rolling with laughter.

And tip they did. They tipped very well.

Photo by Drew Cothern

None of these interactions have ever escalated to violence, but I can honestly say that the years of working in the Quarter has had an effect on me. I don't take shit, and though I will work to avoid it, I'm ready for violence should violence come. The Quarter can be a violent place, after all, and being able to stand your ground is necessary to survive.

Though no violence has come to me, I have witnessed it coming to others. Sometimes, unfortunately, in front of my tour group.

I was standing outside MRB on St. Phillip Street with a group one November evening and I had to pause my story as a cop, an ambulance, and a firetruck went screaming down lower Decatur. I wondered what the matter was, but I didn't worry for long. A moment later, as we rounded the corner onto Decatur, I saw the source of the commotion.

It was a gutterpunk, sitting halfway up the block on the curb, and he was being attended to by a medic. Blood gushed down the side of the gutterpunk's face, but I couldn't see its source due to his thick, blonde dreadlocks and the medic attending him blocking my view.

As we approached, I heard the medic say, "Okay, man, we have to take you in to get you stitched up."

The gutterpunk nodded grimly before replying, "Well...should I get my ear?"

He turned and pointed and I saw it. Not a piece, not a part, no. *His entire right ear had been severed and was lying behind him on the sidewalk.*

Which put me in an awkward position. Do I stop the tour and turn around? Do I do as I typically do and try to ignore it and keep on my route? *How does one simply ignore a severed human ear?* Luckily, I didn't have to make that choice. Another paramedic saw us coming, and like an angel of god, swooped in and rescued the ear, getting it out of sight. The only ones to see it were me and four frat boys walking behind me.

One of them didn't handle it well. I'd never seen anyone literally turn green before, but he did, having to lean on one of his bros to keep steady as we continued down the block. After he stopped gagging and caught his breath, he said to me, his voice shaking, "Did...did you see that guy's *ear?*"

Trying my best to maintain composure, I smiled at him and said, "Oh. First ear, huh?"

Photo by Drew Cothern

One question I am often asked is, "What's the weirdest thing you've seen in the French Quarter?" You'd think a whole human ear lying - like *Blue Velvet* - on the sidewalk would be it, but no. Friends, I have seen things that would make you laugh, make you cry, and scenes that would turn your hair white. But the weirdest thing came, happily, not while I was on tour, but after I'd had a late night that had turned into an early morning in the Quarter.

It was nearing seven o'clock and the sun was coming up and I was sobering up and it was time to go home. I'd parked my car on St. Peter Street, and as I walked towards it, I saw something unexpected down the block. Now, those of us that are in the Quarter every day expect the unexpected, but this was beyond that.

Down the block, I saw a man. Wearing a blue dress. Squatting like a bird on top of an orange Prius. As I got closer, details of this scene started to become clear. His thin, yellow hair was standing out at odd angles and he was gnawing on the crust of old pizza the way a dog does a bone. I noticed there was a puddle of vomit on the hood of the car. About half a block away from him, we locked eyes and I realized with horror what he was doing.

HE WAS FUCKING HIMSELF WITH THE ANTENNA OF THE PRIUS.

We both screamed. He hurled the crust at me before reaching into the greasy pizza box beside him for more ammunition. I hastily apologized. What else could I do? I apologized for interrupting him and said I would go to the next block.

Blurred for your protection – Photo by Drew Cothern

You probably don't believe me. I wouldn't, if I were you. I couldn't believe what I'd seen myself and tour guides, after all, are known to indulge in hyperbole. But it did happen, and I knew that no matter how insistent I was about what I had seen, no one would believe me. As I shakily opened my car door and closed it behind me, I had a realization. In order to leave the Quarter, I would have to drive down St. Peter Street. I would have to drive right past him. My phone was at less than 5% battery. Just enough. The video I took that morning is proof, friends, that you should *always* believe your tour guide because, in the French Quarter at least, the truth truly is stranger than any fiction we could ever dream up on our own.

ANECDOTE: HOPE IN THE FRENCH QUARTER
- *Charmaine Swan Rich*

Today I went for a walk. Because of the Covid-19 Quarantine, I had not been to the French Quarter in a month - which was weird since I am a tour guide and work in the quarter.

Today, the French Quarter was quiet, still and empty. It really freaked me out at first. Then, after a few quiet moments...I felt Her. The City. She is still here, just sometimes She has to recharge Her strength, Her energy.

I felt Her calmness. Her silence. And She was breathing. As I walked around thru the silence I felt Her love - "I am still here, just resting" is what I felt in my heart. But, I still wished I could hear something other than silence with my ears... if only..... Something....the kids hitting the buckets, the clop, clop of the mules, the horns playing....oh the horns...the music... that would help.

As I walked down St. Ann Street and Pere Antoine Alley I guess She heard me. Through the deafening silence I heard him... the guy I had heard him thousands of times, in the same place, by Cafe Du Monde. I walked by him, actually ran by him when I was late for a tour, but now, my heart exploded and tears came to my eyes.... "This little light of mine, I 'm gonna let it shine..."

He was here, singing and clapping, as he always did. It's the "guy that only knows three songs and only about four lines in each song!" And he is here, with his tip bucket - singing!!!!

After I took this picture of Cafe Du Monde, I went over to him and gave him, well, let's just say, it was more than a dollar. He looked at me, right in my eyes and had tears in his eyes - "oh, oh, wow! Thank you ma'am! You spent me out! I can go have lunch now!" Not expecting this, I stumbled with my words, saying "oh, good, stay safe, have a good day!" He got on his bike and took off.

I can't explain the loving, happy, feeling deep in my heart that made me feel warm and fuzzy all over. With what is going on now, She gave me all that I needed... and then I gave that to someone else... and all I am gonna say is "This little light of mine, I'm gonna let it shine...."

11

HURRICANE WARNING
Ariadne Blayde

In my experience, there are two types of tour guides. You've got the ones who prefer small groups so they can lean in close, make chit chat, get to know everybody; these guides basically treat the tour as an informal stroll, a conversation between friends. And then you have prima donnas like me, who call it "My Tour" with capital letters like it's the newest hottest off-Broadway event of the season and demand as large an audience as possible. In my case, My Tour is a one-woman theatrical performance complete with perfectly-crafted turns of phrase, accents, and occasional sections of mime. Horribly cheesy or breathtakingly compelling? I don't give a shit, really, but my tour guests usually tip well enough that I feel good about how I've chosen to use my theatre degree.

 On the night in question (a balmy evening in early March, if I recall correctly) only about a dozen people showed up for the 6:00 Ghost Tour. Some tour guides would be happy to have a small group, but I was not. What star likes a tiny audience? Having a small group makes my scenery-chewing appear awkward and over-the-top, and requires me to tone the tour down to a conversation by going off my usual script. I can't turn on tour-autopilot when I have a small group; I have to actually *work* at my job, and who wants to do that? I almost turned down the tour, but this was immediately post-Mardi Gras and I had some poor spending decisions to make up for.

I stood next to the ticket seller for half an hour before the tour as the customers trickled in. They included: five French-speaking Canadians, a nice stocky couple from Texas or Florida (I can never distinguish nor remember; tourists from these states are equally unpleasant), another nondescript family or two from I don't know where, two exuberant young women of color, and a 25 year old white girl all by herself. The minutes ticked by and I prayed that more would show up. But it was a slow night, and a Tuesday, and I knew I'd just have to work with what I'd been given. At 5:55 I put on my lipstick and at 6:00 I led them away down the sidewalk, already cranky.

At 6:03, it started to rain.

I am usually prepared for rain. I keep a small umbrella in my bag, and as long as it starts raining before the tour begins, we're good to go: the tourists understand that the tour will continue rain or shine, and have taken the time to buy ponchos or umbrellas. But when it starts raining *after* our start time? Bad, bad news. They're not prepared for it. Doesn't matter that they all keep devices in their pockets that can predict the weather; if it's not precipitating when the tour starts and then starts to rain halfway in, they are all 1) terrified, 2) unprepared, and 3) mad at me, since I am, as they always seem to think,, single-handedly responsible for the quality of their New Orleans experience.

I stopped in a different spot than usual so that they could huddle under a small overhang and rushed through my intro, prepared for an already difficult small-group tour to be made more difficult by the rain. But, surprisingly, my introduction went better than I expected. There's a very interesting phenomenon in tour groups, wherein one or two people with a bad vibe can bring down the whole group, and one or two people with a good vibe can elevate the experience for everyone. This tour seemed to be trending toward the latter; the two young women of color were clearly prepared to have a wonderful time, and their enthusiasm was infectious. I apologized for the rain and told the group I hoped they were up for an adventure. "We ain't sugar, we ain't gonna melt!" one of the young women called in response, raising her drink. Some of the other group members laughed and nodded.

How 'bout that, I mused to myself. *Might not be such a bad tour after all.* I breezed through the rules -- one benefit of a small group is that you don't have to be such a stickler about crowd control -- and gave my usual teasing guidelines about drinking, which of course is allowed on the tour as long as it doesn't get out of hand. "Don't get wasted, that's not fun for anyone but you," is my usual line. "I'm looking at y'all with the two-for-one hurricanes," I said, nodding toward the pair of women and single girl, who were all holding pleasantly pink drinks in go-cups. The bar next door offers buy-one-get-one hurricanes for our customers, so the pair of young women had split the deal and each had one. But the solo white girl had apparently decided to drink both herself; one of them was free, after all, so she was double-fisting, one hurricane in each hand. They laughed at my joke and promised to behave.

I launched into my first story and the pair of young women continued to be interested, engaged and talkative. In a big group this can be a problem -- "This is not a conversation," I often have to remind drunken dads who want to interject comments every three sentences -- but in small groups a little back-and-forth with the group can work. I found myself enjoying the conversational tour style that I normally hate so much, and the rain didn't seem to be bothering the group at all. If anything, it seemed to have created a sense of camaraderie. Two teenage boys from separate families seemed to have a snarky teenage-boy thing going, and the solo white girl had jumped onto the duo's vibe train. As we walked to our next stop I heard her laughing and joking with them in the way young women often do in bar bathroom lines, tipsy and quick to make friends with strangers. She had finished her first hurricane and was onto her second, which honestly should have been a red flag, but I was just pleased that they all seemed to be having a good time.

The rain picked up. I did an excellent job keeping the group tucked away under balconies, but I myself got soaked as I stood in the street to deliver the stories. By our third stop, the downpour showed no sign of ceasing and the temperature had dropped ten degrees. I was freezing, and I could tell the group was becoming uncomfortable. I wrapped up the story at the LaLaurie Mansion a little more quickly than usual and hustled them toward the bar where we always take a break, eager to warm up.

On the walk I chatted with the three young women, who had become a unit. I asked the white girl what brought her to town; by now she was quite tipsy and all she could tell me was that she was here with her "woo-woo girls." She referred to her fiancée several times, and I was able to piece together that she was in town for a bachelorette party: her own. "Where are your friends?" I asked, and she said they would all be arriving tomorrow. She stumbled on the sidewalk and one of the duo caught her arm and pulled her close. I looked down at her hand and saw she had sucked down most of her second hurricane in the last 15 minutes. This was an alarming development.

"Make sure she gets some water at the bar," I whispered to the other ladies, and they nodded.

Across the street from the bar I told the group where they could buy ponchos and dismissed them for a ten minute break, then hurried around the corner to my car to get my rain jacket. I was deeply chilled and felt much better after putting it on.

When we returned from our break, the rain had slowed but the white girl was visibly very drunk. She interjected slurred comments as I spoke, but it wasn't cute anymore. "You have to be quiet, honey," I told her in the same voice a kindergarten teacher might use. The other women were now firmly entrenched on either side of her, steadying her as she swayed and murmuring to her in hushed voices to keep her under control.

You may have heard of the famous drink called a "hurricane," invented in New Orleans at the popular Irish tavern Pat O'Brien's in the 1940's. It consists of 2 ounces light rum, 2 ounces dark rum, various fruit juices, and a floater of 151 (which is 75% alcohol by volume). A hurricane is easily two to three times as strong as any other cocktail, and the kicker is, it's sweet and tropical and goes down easy, easy, easy. This girl -- who, might I add, was about 5'2" -- had now had *two* of these concoctions in one hour, and I was pretty sure she hadn't had dinner. Bad news bears.

At our next stop she started vomiting.

Now here's the thing. As a tour guide, I am absolutely allowed to kick disruptively intoxicated people out of the group. I've done it before; the quickest it ever happened was when a basic bro and his girlfriend were so drunk and annoyed at each other they started kicking each other in the shins during my introduction, then made up, which emboldened the dude to start yelling "PENIS" at my next stop. Kicking drunk folks off is not a problem; the boss has our back, and the other patrons are always so relieved to be rid of the assholes that they usually tip better and leave better reviews.

This girl was beyond the point of disruptively drunk. The other group members edged away and tried not to look at her as she huddled behind a car, throwing up pink liquid the same color and consistency as the hurricanes she'd just gulped down. In any other circumstance I'd have kicked her out of the group, but I realized with horror there was absolutely no way I could do that. She was all alone, not only in the group but *in the whole city*. Her other bachelorettes hadn't arrived yet. This girl was tiny, wasted, and sending her out into the streets of the Quarter by herself was out of the question.

I announced an emergency break and ran across the street to the coffee shop to get her a bottle of water, while the two young ladies held her hair and patted her back. The French Canadians announced politely that they would be leaving, and I felt a surge of frustration; they were nearly half the group, and clearly did not intend to tip me before they departed.

When I got back from the coffee shop the girl was apologizing through a haze of tears, horribly embarrassed. "It's okay, it's okay," her new friends said reassuringly as they patted her back. "Happens to everybody. You're gonna be okay."

I very frankly told the rest of the group that I had no choice but to keep the girl with us, for her own safety. They were understanding enough. We were almost finished, anyway -- just a couple more stops. During the next story the girl made a valiant effort to seem like she was interested and paying attention, nodding vigorously at every sentence and occasionally taking breaks to step away and vomit. She seemed to get most of it out, and was marginally more sober by the time we got to our last stop. I rushed through my sleep-paralysis story and sagged with relief when I finally got to my outro, possibly more desperate than I'd ever been for a tour to end. Tips? Abominable. Ones and fives, probably fifteen bucks total; normally I hit at least $60, even with small groups.

The other group members wandered away, leaving me, the young ladies and our drunken charge alone on the wet sidewalk. She was now openly crying, horrified at her own behavior, and the young ladies -- who, I was now convinced, were literal angels sent from heaven -- soothed her and tried to cheer her up. "Hey, there's no crying in baseball!" one said. "Yeah, chin up, girl, you're gonna be okay in no time."

"She's gotta get back to her hotel," one of them said to me, and I nodded. "Girl, where you staying?"

We got the information out of her after a few tries: a hotel in the Central Business District, on the other side of the French Quarter.

"I guess we ought to put her in an Uber or something?"

I shook my head. "Nah, she'll barf. And that's a giant fee."

By now it was clear what I had to do. "I've got this from here. Y'all go enjoy the rest of your night," I said, thanking them profusely. "I literally could not have gotten through this tour without you."

"Oh, it was no big deal! Just hope she's okay tomorrow," they laughed.

Can I actually give you a hug?" I asked, and embraced them each. Never in my five years as a tour guide had I been so grateful for someone in my group.

"Oh! I'm so sorry, we don't have any cash to tip you," one said.

"My god, are you kidding?" I laughed. "I'm the one who should be tipping you."

I said goodnight to them and they went off laughing and cheerful, totally unphased by the last two hours' nightmarish events.

"Come on, babe, you're coming with me," I said, hauling the white girl to her feet.

"Where are we going?"

"The only place you *can* go, honey. Back to your hotel to sleep this off."

I took her to my car -- my most prized possession, by the way, a convertible red Mini Cooper -- and got her buckled in. "I'm gonna drive you back, okay? Barf out the window if you need to."

"I'm so sorry," she burbled through hiccups and more tears. "This is so-- so embarrass-- ing. I'm not like this, I promise. I'm not this-- this kind of ind-- individual."

"Happens to everybody," I said. "I'm just glad I'm here to make sure you're safe."

Her cheeks filled with vomit as we hit a pothole. "Out the window, out the window!" I hollered, lowering it for her. But short as she was, she wasn't able to get her head out the window far enough for a clear shot , so she opened the passenger door a crack.

"Woah woah woah! Don't open the door!" I said, rolling up to a stoplight. She spat vomit out the gap and wiped her lips. "Don't do that again, okay? And put your seatbelt back on!"

She did it again five minutes later, luckily when the car was stopped, and then again one or two more times. Between the constant door-opening and endless apologizing, my patience quickly wore thin. Add to that the fact that it was still raining and visibility wasn't great, and the ten minute drive felt like it took thirty. After navigating through a frustrating series of one way streets I finally pulled up to her hotel.

"Okay. We're here. This is it, right? This is where you're staying?"

"Yes," she said vaguely. "I think so."

"Get some room service once you get up there. You have to eat."

She started to cry again. "This is the worst night ever. I'm such an idiot."

"Hey," I said, putting a hand on her shoulder. "No it's not. Your friends aren't here yet, nobody has to know. Tomorrow's a new day, okay? And now you've learned your lesson, so you'll have a much better time for the rest of the week. And you really will have the best time. It's hard not to, in this city," I smiled.

She sniffled and nodded, then started wailing again. "You're such a saint. And I'm the worst tour customer ever."

I laughed, considering this. "Well, maybe. But at least you have the self-awareness to acknowledge it. Most of them don't," I said, remembering Penis-shouting guy and his awful girlfriend.

I jotted down my number on a slip of paper. "This is my name and number, okay? Text me if you need anything. And for God's sake, do not leave this hotel until morning."

"I won't," she promised.

She clumsily gathered her things and got out of the car. I made sure she hadn't left anything behind, watched as she stumbled into the hotel past the totally-unphased doorman, and drove away through the rain, hoping it would wash away the trail of vomit down the side of my car door.

The next day I got a text at 1 pm. "Hello from the most embarrassed person in the world!" it said. We shot a few texts back and forth, she apologized again, I made some jokes to help her feel better. "What's your Venmo?" she asked. "I at least owe you a car wash."

"Oh, don't worry about it," I texted back, hoping she would see through the lie. Sure enough, a few seconds later my phone made that delightful cash-register sound. Fifty bucks. My eyes popped with money signs, like a cartoon character's. I thanked her and told her it wasn't necessary.

"By the way, I loved your tour," she said. "What I remember of it, anyway. You're really good at what you do."

Hell yes I'm good at what I do, I thought, immediately and gratefully transferring the fifty bucks to my empty bank account. "Take care of yourself," I texted back. "And enjoy the hell out of New Orleans."

My first Halloween in this city, I "pregamed" with a hurricane and ended up so drunk that I had to miss the big party and go home, sobbing, at eight o'clock. On New Years' eve two weeks after I turned 26 I got so drunk that I wandered down the train tracks by the river and then let myself into the tour company's storage closet and fell asleep, my boyfriend frantically searching for me all the while.

I've thrown up in people's yards, cried in bar bathrooms, become overly friendly with strangers. What woman hasn't, in her twenties? I don't hold a thing against that girl, and I'm glad I could get her home safe. Countless women have done the same for me. She seemed like a sweet, responsible person whose overdrinking was an accident, and we've all been there. Hell, many of us have indulged in overdrinking on purpose, on the regular. I hope she learns her lesson and doesn't make that mistake again

Of course, some people never grow out of the binge-drinking and bad-decision-making phase. We get a lot of visitors like that in New Orleans, some of them well into their 40's and 50's and 60's and still struggling with finding and managing their own limits. I grew out of my unhappy relationship with alcohol; I had to. It would be impossible to walk the streets of the French Quarter every night if I didn't have a handle on myself, my drinking, my coping skills. I know how incredibly lucky I am to live the life I do, and have the job I do. And the reality is, sometimes the cost of that is dealing with people who aren't so lucky. People whose lives are hard and boring and painful, people who need an escape. For some, New Orleans is the only place they really get to let go. And whenever I have an inconvenient, annoying, or downright exhausting experience with someone who has let go a little too much, I try to remind myself how fortunate I am to be in New Orleans telling ghost stories for a living.

No amount of bachelorette barf can take that away from me.

So it's a busy weekend before Halloween Saturday night at the Dungeon. They usually are. But this one, even more so because it's also Voodoo Fest weekend and the city is packed.

I'm working the downstairs bar, which is my domain, when I notice our doorman, Alan, is waving, trying to get my attention and yelling "1942! 1942!" At first I thought he was having a stroke, or something, so I yelled back "1942 what? I follow his gaze to find Dave Grohl and his entourage taking a seat at the bar. Okay. Got it.

Now, to Alan, 1942 actually means something. You see Alan was working at Yo Mama's Burgers on St. Ann one day a few years back, when Dave Grohl walked in and sat down at the bar. The Foo Fighters were in town filming Sonic Highways across the street at Preservation Hall and he came in for drinks. They did this a lot all over the Quarter.

Ironically, the bartender didn't know who Dave Grohl was, so when he ordered shots of Don Julio Tequila 1942, she says "Hey, this is $20 a shot. You sure you can afford this?" And he smiled and replied "Yeah, I got it covered." So Alan remembered this and getting a little stunned and flustered that Dave had just walked into The Dungeon, that's apparently all he could get to come out of his mouth.

Now I have to say, working at a place like the Dungeon, you get to meet a lot of celebrities, and, over the years, let's just say I have a really long list. But Dave Grohl, he's in a class unto himself. He is literally the coolest person I have ever met. He's so humble and grounded. He's very generous. He looks you in the eye when he talks to you. For me it was magical.

In the midst of everything that's going on, there's a group of people in the cage. One had a ball cap on. Now I don't get star struck often, and I never do this, but I went over to the people in the cage and said "Dave Grohl is here!" And they laughed and it was fine. I guess I let my excitement get the best of me,

But as the night progressed, with everything that was going on, the people in the cage began to irritate me. So, about an hour had transpired, when I finally got pissed off at something that they did, went back to them and said "Alright, you guys are gonna have to pay up, or leave, or do something, because you just can't sit around and stare at Dave Grohl all night." To my surprise they were actually really nice about it. Some are not. They ended up leaving and I kind of felt like I'd maybe been a little bit of a jerk, but, oh well.

Then I find out that the guy in the ball cap was Tom Fucking Morello of Rage Against the Machine. Whoa! And I remember his face when I told him that he couldn't be staring at Dave Grohl. What was that look? Shock? Amusement? I can't quite recall. But, in my defense, he kind of was just sitting there staring at Dave Grohl. In retrospect, I'm sure they knew each other and I'm sure that's why he was staring, but he was kind of incognito in a ball cap, looking like an average Joe, and Dave Grohl was getting all the attention.

So, that's my tale of how I rescued Dave Grohl from Tom Morello at the Dungeon. Just remember, not all heroes wear capes. Some of us wear horns.

Photo by Rachel Lockett

12

THE DISAPPEARING FACE

Stella Salmen

Muriel's Restaurant: Jackson Square

Muriel's Restaurant is one of the most popular haunted locations for ghost tours in the city. Having been heavily damaged by the Good Friday Fire of 1788, it was sold to a wealthy man… with a gambling problem. As one would expect in a ghost story, the tragic events were, play poker, bet mansion, lose mansion, commit suicide.

Although his family had to depart the mansion to satisfy the gambling debt, his spirit remained. He also took issue with the location being turned into a restaurant, as he mistook well-dressed people partaking of fine food and spirits as being parties… he loved parties, and evidently felt insulted that he was not invited. The more successful the restaurant, the more active the hauntings… until a psychic medium communicated his reasons to the owners. To make him feel more welcome, there is a special "Ghost Table" in the old carriageway. Private dining for our restless spirit. Groups visiting can look down the long hall and view the table from the street. They also get the opportunity to take pictures.

I always caution my guests that the plexiglass on the gate is quite warped and scratched, so many times "anomalies" that appear in photos can be attributed to that, but not always.

I ask my guests to wait until we take our mid-tour bar break to show me odd photos, because if I looked at them after each stop we would never get through the tour. Yet on this occasion I made an exception.

Stepping down from the carriageway to allow my guests to get photos, I wait for my group to gather. One woman who had been front and center, and got her pictures right away, walked up scrolling through her shots, and suddenly froze in place with her eyes as wide as saucers! I had suggested using the "burst" setting on phone cameras... it takes 10-12 pictures in a fraction of a second, and can capture images that pass too quickly for the human eye to see. She had taken my advice, and on seeing her shock, I asked to see what she captured. Why not... others were still at the doorway taking photos. Fully expecting to see just an odd reflection, I instead got quite a shock!

She scrolled through the pictures:

Table, Table, Table, FACE, Table, Table...

I physically jumped!

Ok, people were gathering, and I told her that I really wanted to see that again when we got to the bar break.

3 stories later we break, and I ask the woman to show me that photo burst again. She was a bit nervous, but also glad to have confirmation.

Opened the photo series, and:

Table, Table, Table, Table, Table, Table, Table... it was gone.

My favorite picture with Stella, stealing her soul, October 2016

13

BRINGING THEM BACK WITH YOU

When dealing with the paranormal, especially as much as we do, there is always a very real possibility of spirit attachment. My wife and I learned this in a very real way after our visit in 2005. We were living in Maryland at the time and had friends from California and Maryland join us in New Orleans for a benchmark vow renewal ceremony and to celebrate Mardi Gras. This was the same visit I discuss towards the end of Chapter One where we experienced the balcony chair spirit activity at the Bourbon Orleans Hotel.

Our group took a fascinating cemetery tour to St. Louis Cemetery No. 1 and I was immediately hooked on the cemetery culture here. The cities of the dead. Our guide was great. Polite, informative and very proud of the city. It made quite an impression on me. He also mentioned that he was a Voodoo practitioner and I watched as our group squirmed a little.

You see, the only thing we knew about Voodoo was what we had seen in the movies, with zombies, frightening potion induced rituals and frantic orgies. At the Marie Laveau tomb he dispelled a lot of those myths and explained the religious aspects and practices in a way that relaxed some of the tension in the group. Towards the end he invited those of us who were interested to attend a blessing ceremony at the Voodoo Spiritual Temple and Cultural Center on Rampart Street, to be conducted by Priestess Miriam. I'll admit, I was a little nervous, but also very intrigued, so our group decided to do it. I believe a little more than half the tour participated.

Once we got inside Priestess Miriam greeted us and I remember thinking "what a beautiful soul". She radiated inner peace and immediately put us at ease. We all sat in a semi-circle while she swept the negative energies away from us and replaced them with good. If remember correctly, we were given these little sachet type bags, containing herbs to keep us safe and protected.

Back in the room I promptly tossed them in my suitcase and forgot about them, until we returned home a few days later. That evening, back in our own bed, I settled in to begin reading a new book I'd purchased during our visit entitled "Searching for Spirits by Kalila Smith". If you'd told me then that 12 years later I would be working with her at Haunted History Tours, I would have said you were crazy. Seems the fates knew what they were doing even then.

Around 11:30pm I turned out the light and we settled in to sleep. Having drifted off, we were both awakened with a start by someone pounding on our front door. I glanced at the clock and it was straight up 12 midnight. Grabbing my robe, I figured it must be an emergency of some sort for one of our neighbors to be acting that way. As soon as my foot hit the landing at the bottom of the stairs, the pounding stopped. I turned on the porch light, quickly opened the door and found… that there was no one there. Not a soul and not a sound.

I walked out to the sidewalk, listening for noises. Nothing. I checked around the house. Again, nothing. Scratching my head, I went back inside and up to bed where my wife was waiting, sitting on her side of the bed. "What was it?" she asked. "No idea. Maybe kids, who knows." I turned my bedside table lamp off and we both snuggled back into bed.

That's when the oddest thing happened. The overhead chandelier lights in our bedroom came on. By themselves. No. I'm not kidding. We both immediately sat up in bed and I have to admit, my heart was pumping and my mind was racing a mile a minute. A knock at midnight, our lights coming on by themselves. What the hell was happening? Then my wife, who is not into this paranormal stuff even a little bit, spoke out loud and said "whoever you are, I don't want you here. We don't want any trouble. Please leave peacefully." Two minutes later the lights turned off and in the next seven years of our living there, it never happened again,

We may never know what it was, but I felt somehow that we had dodged a bullet. A few days later, cleaning out the rest of the stuff from my suitcase, I found those two gris gris bags that we were given at the Voodoo Shop. Do I think they were responsible for what happened that night? On the contrary, I think they may have protected us and I had a new respect for a religion that was very foreign to the way I was raised. But, as I would find out later, this little incident was a walk in the park compared to what some experience.

Shadow Figure Art Concept by Drew Cothern

Remember earlier in the book, when I promised you another creepy Dungeon occurrence? I saved the best, or scariest, for last. Here goes.

At one of my tour stops, The Chartres House, on a Monday evening in May 2019, I ran into two couples from SoCal who were on my Sunday late tour the night before. They were eating dinner and as soon as they saw me, they started frantically waving me over.

Smiling and happy to see them, I walked over and asked them how they'd been and if they'd had fun last night. The husband of one of the couples admitted that they had a "really rough night". "Too many Dragon's Blood shots?" I asked, thinking they were suffering from hangovers. "No", he replied, "We believe dark spirits attached themselves to us at The Dungeon and followed us back to our hotel." Um, what?

Apparently, after I left them at The Dungeon at the end of the tour the husband of the couple said he kept seeing a shadow figure hovering by them when they were at one of the upstairs bars. This went on for quite some time. Where ever they would go, it seemed to follow them. Hanging back, but just on the edge of his peripheral vision. At one point he said he saw it lunge towards them from behind and it scared him so badly that they decided to leave and go back to their hotel.

Once there, they brushed their teeth, got ready for bed and kind of nervously laughed about the tour and the weirdness they experienced at The Dungeon.

They crawled in bed, kissed and turned off the light, and that's when his wife saw what appeared to be the shadow figure of a man standing by the end of the bed watching them. She screamed and her husband immediately turned on the light and the figure disappeared. I'd like to note that at this point of recounting the story, both the husband and wife started getting teary eyed and shaking a little. I told them to be calm, that they would be okay and I would help them. He continued.

Turning off the light again, they discovered that there were now two shadow figures in the room, one male and the other female. The wife told me that at one point she felt what she described as "an invisible woman" crawling on top of her, starting with her feet. She could feel her hands and the shape and weight of a woman's body on top of her and felt as if her own body was "frozen." Again she screamed, her husband turned on the light and the sensation of being pinned lifted. Surprisingly, that's not the really terrifying part.

The husband said that they turned on all the lights and eventually drifted off to sleep. When he woke up it was daylight and he was relieved that they had somehow survived the night. And, as he turned to look over at his sleeping wife he felt a presence beside him who leaned in and whispered in his ear "slit her throat."

It upset him so badly that he started crying and he jumped out of the bed, his legs collapsing underneath him. His wife, hearing the commotion, woke up wondering what was wrong.

He said it took him a while to even find himself able to utter the words to her to describe not only what had happened, but the grim task he was instructed to accomplish. It took about five minutes, and once he was able to tell her, then she became afraid of him. I mean, these two kids literally had a night from hell.

They were still visibly shaken and teary eyed telling me the story. I referred them to a friend who could help them smudge and protect themselves and showed them the protection ring I wear on my tours. This is, hands down, truly one of the most bizarre and terrifying experiences I've encountered while doing tours here.

Amanda showing the shadow figures who is boss at the Dungeon

ANECDOTE: THE HOUND FROM HELL

Remember, my bartender friend Rachel, the one who saved Dave Grohl? Well she started having odd things happen with her cell phone thru the month of October, 2018. She usually keeps it under the counter at the bar next to the register where it had mysteriously started taking pictures on its own, of the shelves under the bar. These were not photo bursts, but photos taken at different intervals throughout her shift. In one instance there were 13 pictures taken over the span of an hour, even though her phone was locked and no apps were open.

The last time it happened was on October 31st, 2018, and she heard it click. She grabbed her phone and went out to the courtyard and there was one picture that had not only taken itself, but it was linking to Instagram. It was trying to upload the photo to the page of some chick from Romania, who she didn't know. She killed that from happening and that's when she noticed something in the pic. Something that had not been in any of the others. She zoomed in and this is what she found. Hound from hell, anyone?

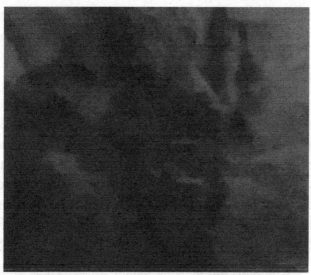

Demon Dog – Photo by Rachel Lockett

14

NIGHT STALKERS

Jonathan Weiss

I've always loved the city of New Orleans, and of all the things I've loved, more than any is how different she is at night than from the day. While it has that feel now, in the days before Katrina it was truly remarkable, and something that was easily experienced.

Over and over, the new to the city, the inexperienced, the tourist would find themselves in an area that they couldn't recognize, the brows would furrow, they would look again and again over their shoulders in trepidation and worry, sure that they would remember something, and more shaken when for all their efforts, it only seemed more alien.

While we residents of the old city knew our locations, the feeling of something terrible, something... watching was always there, lurking just out of view. It's so simple, yet so strange how, like a Stephen King novel, the benign just starts to twist until what was something charming begins to fill you with dread, and the realization comes: you're in someplace *different*. And something simple and bizarre happened to me soon after my most recent return to the city.

In 2003, I was working as a bartender on Bourbon Street as my main gig - and no, that's definitely not the weird part - guides used to apprentice for their positions (and generally you're not considered local till you've done your time on Bourbon!).

I would go to work at 9pm, and often not leave till 9am in the days when the city didn't stop. While this being the case during the weekends, on slow nights I was done in the dead hours, just after 3am, when the city oftentimes finally slows into an uneasy slumber.

I lived on the downriver lakeside of the Quarter, on Burgundy and Governor Nicholls, the area of the city that things traditionally happen to tour guides. The things that make *us* uncomfortable, the things that even *we* don't want to talk about and usually then amongst ourselves alone and usually while drinking.

I'd left work early that night, and was walking the shadowy blocks home feeling quite satisfied with myself, money in my pocket, breathing in the rich thick air and relishing in the relatively cool, jasmine-scented night. And as I neared my home, I saw something moving in concert with me to my left along St. Philip street - turning my head I realized that it was a cat, one of the many ferals that have always hung around our ancient port, and it was walking along the line of cars, keeping pace with me, head low-slung, eyes locked on me.

Photo by Chastity Yvonne

I thought that was kind of cool, really. Like I was being escorted home by a fellow gentleman of the Quarter, like-knowing-like, as it were, and I smiled and greeted him. He didn't respond.

As I neared Burgundy, I realized that he'd been joined by another, and they were leaping from car to car, gateway top to walk, pacing, and... watching. When I turned onto Burgundy, and was within a block of my home, the traffic pattern changed and the cars were now on the right, so these two abandoned the cars, trotted across the road and began to slink along the shadowy doorways, never turning their gaze.

Photo submitted by Elliot Gorton

I admit, at that point I was getting a bit unnerved, but continued along towards home just ahead, when a motion caught my eye to the right - a third had joined the first two, it was now keeping pace on the right, eyes glowing in the pale streetlights.

Then I spied another, this one crouched and moving furtively along underneath the cars, glaring and glaring. I stopped. They stopped. I moved, they followed, unblinking and bearing what now began to dawn on me was a fascination, a cold malice in their narrowed eyes.

Suddenly I realized that the breeze had died, and how very still it had all become, seeming as if everything was holding its breath, frozen in place and desperately trying not to be noticed. A stillness of *age*.

I looked ahead, and as the hairs on the back of my neck began to stir, a large, scarred male slowly strolled into the middle of Burgundy Street, for all the world as if he owned it, sat, curled his tail around his legs and *glared*. I didn't want to, I guess because I *knew* already what I'd see, but slowly turned around to look behind me. And crouching there were two others who'd moved into the street behind me, tails twitching. And in a feeling I can't easily describe I understood something that must have been a familiar fear of our oldest ancestors: I was being stalked.

I immediately broke into a run towards the iron gate of my old home, shouting and waving my arms like a lunatic, but not looking back at whatever might have been behind me - slammed through it, and crashed it closed, raced upstairs to my tiny garret apartment, and looked into the lamp lit street below. Then double checked the lock on the door, and drew the curtains tight.

Photo by Jonathan Weiss

Because there they all sat. Staring upwards. Right into my eyes.

Truth.

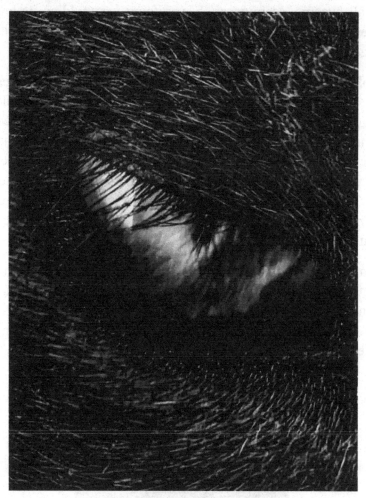

Photo by Kelly Mcmillian

15

BLIND AMBITION
Rose Sinister

I qualified for my City of New Orleans Tour Guide License in September 0f 2013, but I didn't get a chance to perform my first ghost tour until mid-October, in the lead-up to Halloween. That's the way it is in my profession; the new guides start at the bottom of the seniority totem pole and either take the tours that the more experienced guides don't want, or get assigned the last dredges of tourists who show up at the last minute on particularly busy nights in the high season.

The months that follow Halloween in New Orleans are *not* the high season for tourists. The weather cools, the revelers leave, and work is scarce until the lead up to Mardi Gras starts.

All of this to say that I was still pretty green, as far as experience goes, by the time Carnival was about to hit us full-force in the face in early March, 2014. The weather was cold, the streets were crowded and polluted and *filthy:* I mean, really, truly, filthy, saturated with every variety of human and animal bodily fluid you can imagine- yes, even that- washed down with stale beer and sickly sweet melted daiquiris.

I'd probably performed fewer than two dozen tours by then, enough to have my stories pretty memorized, but not fluidly. I knew my route well enough, but not intimately. I was getting decent tips, but not great ones.

By this point I'd dealt with a few hecklers and a few belligerent bums, and I'd seen enough poop on the cracked and uneven sidewalks to instantly be able to tell the difference between human and canine. Besides, I'd been a resident of New Orleans for the better part of a decade already, I'd worked in the French Quarter nearly the entirety of that time. I'd seen the Jesus freaks with their bullhorns next to the body-painted naked people covered in beads next to the passed-out Oklahoma tourists on the sidewalk often enough that they hardly registered anymore.

I thought, in my hubris, that I'd seen it all.

Enter Lundi Gras night. That's "Fat Monday" in French but it's only an "official" part of Mardi Gras in New Orleans, and only recently at that. It's basically the night before the last hurrah. The last night to take a ghost tour before Carnival is over for yet another year.

So, despite the chill in the air, the tourists came out in droves, crowding the ticket window on the sidewalk and I watched, bottom of the tour guide totem pole as one, after another, after another full-to-capacity tour group departed along the sidewalk as the clock moved closer to 8 pm. That's when the last ghost tour leaves for the night, and it was looking like another no-work night for me. The crowd along the sidewalk had started to thin, and those of us left over started to pack up the signs and the credit card machines and lock them away for the night.

I don't know if I'm the one who saw them first, or if it was someone else who said, "Oh, *no...*" but we all looked up at once and noticed both groups hurrying down the sidewalk toward what was left of the Haunted History tour setup with the deliberate intention in their step clearly indicating that, while they were late, they expected to be accommodated for a tour.

Two clusters of tourists, arriving at the same time but not together-one cluster of six was a group of fraternity brothers from some university up north, already so drunk that they were slurring their words and complaining that it had taken too long to find our sign-in location.

The other group of tourists, also around a half dozen in number, were also students- of the Ruston Louisiana School for the Blind.

At the last minute, I had my work cut out for me after all. As I straightened my license and prepared to step out with my last-minute cluster of a dozen or so students, roughly half sighted, half blind, I could already hear the groans from some of the frat boys that this was going to *suuuuuck*.

I can't say that I expected much better myself. I'm ashamed to admit that my first thought was selfish, indignant, and downright ableist: what the hell kind of blind person comes out and takes a ghost tour of the French Quarter on one of the busiest nights of the year? And what the hell was I supposed to do, stand in front of buildings they couldn't see and tell them stories of ghost sightings they wouldn't perceive, tell them to take photographs so that maybe, when they went home, they'd find orbs or ectoplasm or some other visual proof of ghosts in the images captured by their cameras?

I arrived at Pirate's Alley, where I normally began my tours, with my mismatched group in tow, and looked down, at the flagstone pavers beneath my feet. I'd often wondered, '*if these stones could talk...*'

And I realized, suddenly, how distinctively different the flagstones of the alleyway were from the other parts of the sidewalk we'd just walked down, and I looked at the canes that my blind tourists were using to navigate the crowds and the filth and the obstacles, and suddenly I thought, "what *better* night than Lundi Gras in the French Quarter, to really put those navigational skills to the test?'

And what better night than this, when I was unlikely to snag any prime real estate for storytelling in front of the most famous buildings anyway, to focus on all the non-visual elements of hauntings and paranormal activity that I'd formally glossed over in my scripted recitations of terrible things happening to terrible people and the terrifying legacies of those long-ago traumas?

New Orleans is for everyone. *Stories* are for everyone. And my job, as a storyteller, isn't a route, static performance about me- my job is to reach people where they are, and communicate to them on the level they best understand, why this history matters, why these stories are important, and why these tragedies are *haunting*.

I'd only really known that in a bland, rather intellectual way before that night.

But what does a haunted house mean, if the visuals are irrelevant? I can describe the texture of stone and peeling paint, the hollow echo of angry voices in the night, the icy cold of ghostly hands wrapped tight around your neck as you are sleeping…

There's the ichorous, palpable, sticky quality of hot blood from a disemboweled Romeos dripping slowly off a cast iron spike above you, the deafening jeers of a mob at an execution, the stench of rotting bodies piled chest high down the street, waiting to be gathered and thrown into the river, or the frigid cold of icy wind and sleet pummeling the naked flesh of a doomed young woman in love, freezing to death on a rooftop on a cold December night.

Storytelling is about creating an image in the mind's eye. You don't need to see in order to experience that, in order to feel that.

There are defining moments in all our lives that indelibly crystalize our values and our ambitions in one fell swoop. I'd never stopped to consider, before that night, how I could- and *should*- strive to make my tours more inclusive and accessible for everyone. But it's a story I bring up every single time a new tour guide asks me for advice about the job.

"Your job is to tell a story. Your performance is not about you. A decade from now, people will probably forget the minutiae of historical details in your stories, so don't get too bogged down in those. Remember, you're in a position to create a memory that someone might carry with them for the rest of their lives, and what they will remember most is how you made them *feel.*"

The blind students loved the tour. The Yankee fraternity brothers loved the tour so much they decided to forgo drinking at the bar break so they didn't get any drunker and miss out on the tour- and that's high praise coming from frat bros in town for Mardi Gras.

I got my tour guide license in September of 2013. But Monday night, March 3rd, 2014, was the night I became a Storyteller.

Rose Sinister in Pirates Alley – Photo by Ryan Miller Lane

In addition to sharing stories with people about the city I love, one of my favorite aspects of being a tour guide is watching the reactions of the tour patrons while I'm espousing some of these truly gruesome tales. For instance, I had one lady burst in to tears in an upstairs event room one evening. She somehow thought that because we were sitting at tables that we were going to have a séance and she was terrified. Even after I assured her several times that that was not going to happen, she continued to be afraid as long as we were in that room.

On another occasion this young lady was absolutely so not digging my recounting of the dark history of torture and execution in Jackson Square. Her friends were so amused by her reactions that they snapped pictures and sent them to me later (see below).

And that was at the very beginning of the tour.

5 Star Review Coming My Way!

My all-time favorite reaction, however, was from a lady from Clemson here with her husband for the division title game against LSU in January of 2020. They were very sweet and her husband, as we were walking between stops, told me that he was a firefighter and his wife was a pharmacist.

A few stops later we're at the Pharmacy Museum and I'm telling the gruesome tale of Dr. Dupas when I look over to see this lady staring at me, wide eyed, and nodding.

Acknowledging her I said, "That's right, you're a Pharmacist aren't you?"

She screamed! Loud. Dropped her drink and stepped back, both hands covering her mouth. Astonishment all over her face. She replied "How did you know?"

Obviously she had not heard us talking earlier.

I looked at her husband and he winked. I replied "The spirits told me." And she literally freaked out. "OMG! That's not possible!"

After a few moments her husband started laughing and said "I told him earlier." After punching him several times in the shoulder and calling him a few choice names we were finally able to settle down get back on track. The whole tour cracked up.

At the end he thanked me and tipped me $100.

Terrorizing your loved ones, it's a service we provide.

16

BAR MON CHER
817 St. Louis St.

Bar Mon Cher was a beautiful little oasis of a bar on busy St. Louis Street between Bourbon and Dauphine. Good drinks, great music and creole atmosphere. It literally transported you back to a simpler time. It's the place where a wonderful burlesque performer by the name of Lefty Lucy captivated us and taught us the joys of Burlesque Bingo. For almost two years, until it changed ownership, Bar Mon Cher was a wonderful stop on my Haunted Pub Crawl. It was also, of course, extremely haunted.

The owner, Jeanette, was kind enough to share a story, and a picture, with me from the day she moved in. She pulled up to the front of the locked and alarmed building and stepped back across the street, to take it all in for a moment, before she turned the key and all the transformational hard work of restoring the interior began. That's when she noticed a lady in a white dress watching her from an upstairs balcony window. But wait, wasn't the building supposed to be empty? Weren't the doors locked and the alarm system set, as promised? Making her way into the building she discovered that all was as it was supposed to be. She unlocked the door, turned off the alarm and headed upstairs to investigate. No one was there. But she had a picture. She had proof.

The Lady in White – Original Picture (left) and Close Up

Unable to let go of the mystery Jeanette did some investigating in the City archives. That's where she found records of a 1800s cabinet maker named Barthelemy who fell into a forbidden love affair with the young slave woman who was purchased by his sister, Madame Bacas, to care for her daughter. The young woman's name was Adalaide.

Barthelemy and Adalaide took up residence at 817 St. Louis in 1822 and lived, with their ten children, on the property for 36 years. Yes, you read that right, ten children. His woodworking shop was downstairs and their residence occupied the upper two floors.

After what we believe to have been a long and happy life, Adalaide, the Matriarch of the house, died in 1855 at the age of 72. But, that doesn't mean she left the property. She apparently continues to watch over her old abode and Jeanette believes that it was her, in the window on that first day, checking out the new owner to see if she met with her approval.

Jeanette continued to draw Adalaide's attentions, and would catch glimpses of Adalaide watching her as she prepared the upstairs room for a party, or accomplished some other task in the bar. She also frequently felt her presence on the staircase and the second floor landing.

Oddly enough, Adalaide would also mimic Jeanette's voice so that employees would think she was talking to them, when Jeanette was actually locked away in the apartment upstairs. The employees would hear her call their name, or ask; "what are you doing?" They would turn around to see, out of the corner of their eye, a fleeting glimpse of who they believed to be Jeanette quickly passing by their station, dressed all in white.

Jeanette witnessed this occurrence for herself one evening during Burlesque Bingo. Honey Tangerine, the performer that evening, was on the stage in between bingo games. She was staring at Jeanette, who was across the bar, maybe 20 feet away, and mouthing "What, Jeanette?" Jeanette just stared at her, dumbfounded, and then watched as the sudden realization crossed Honey's face that Jeanette wasn't saying anything. Honey was hearing Jeanette's voice in her ear, talking to her, while Jeanette was across the bar, too far away for a casual conversation. She was literally hearing Jeanette call her name while watching Jeanette standing silently across room.

We also believe that the lady in white is not the only spirit occupying the building. The door man, Jonathan, would frequently tell me stories of seeing children running up the stairs and of chasing phantom children around the first floor.

The first time it happened he thought somehow someone had managed to sneak past him. He caught a glimpse of them turning the corner of the foyer entering the bar and gave chase, only to find that no one was there. This apparently happened quite often.

We know that four of Adalaide's family members died on the property: Barthelemy, Adalaide and two of their children. One child, Louis, died in infancy and the other, Felix, died at the age of 15 when he tragically drowned in the Mississippi River during a 4th of July celebration.

The casket in the courtyard at Bar Mon Cher

Jeanette, and her staff received a surprising answer to the mystery of the children during a séance that was conducted in September of 2017 where the departed spirits of a woman and two children were contacted who resided on the property.

The séance, conducted by Eevie Ford, Cedric Whittaker and Michael Bill, all outstanding guides and mediums, experienced the sounds of children running on the stairs, a little boy laughing and the strong scent of roses.

The following weekend I brought a tour in and we took a group shot at the bar. There, passing through the top of the picture, were three self-illuminated orbs, moving in unison near the ceiling. When I showed it to Jeanette, she told me about the séance and it all fell in place.

The séance and the three spirts

Another fun Pub Crawl at Bar Mon Cher.

Lefty Lucy calling Burlesque Bingo to passersby.

Your Hostess Jeanette (on left)

ANECDOTE: THE LADY WITH HER HUSBAND IN AN URN

During the summer of 2019 I was conducting another Haunted Pub Tour and all twenty eight of us were lining up to check into The Dungeon. Being the host, I stand at the door as my tour patrons check in to make sure there are no problems with IDs, etc.

I happened to look down the line of my group and noticed a lady, perhaps mid-sixties, standing in the middle of my group, clutching and Urn. Yep. Like somebody's ashes inside, type urn. I promptly got her up to the front of our group, because we were going to be a while checking in.

She thanked me and asked Alan, the door guy for a favor. He nodded. She stated that the Dungeon was her and her husband's favorite bar for decades and decades. Every time they visited New Orleans they would hang out here. Sadly he had passed over the summer and his ashes were in that urn. She wanted to know if it was okay to dump her husband's ashes into the palm tree planter next to the entry door. It was his dying wish.

I was standing there wide-eyed and a little emotional, when Alan shrugged, very nonchalantly, in typical NOLA fashion, like people ask this type of thing every day, and said "Sure, I don't care, go ahead". I was kind of floored, but also thought it was very cool.

So my tour group and I watched solemnly as this lady dumped her husband's ashes in that planter. It is my understanding that the ashes of three more departed souls have joined him at the time of this writing. God, I love this town.

17

MAY BAILEY'S BAR
415 Dauphine Street

May Baily's is one of my absolute favorite stops on our Haunted Pub Crawl. The hotel bar for the Dauphine Orleans Hotel, this place is brimming with New Orleans brothel history and boasts of four very diverse and active spirits! This is a must stay location if you're looking to immerse yourself in the haunted lore of the city. Not surprising, I've also had more than a few ghostly encounters at this bar.

The first was in July of 2017. I had a full tour of 28 people and as we entered the bar, I recall one lady doing a Face Book live video, sharing the experience with her kids back home that they were entering a haunted bar. I thought it was cute. We finished the tour with no incidents and then a few days later I got a call from our front office, that one of my weekend tour patrons had called and left a message asking for me to contact them right away, that they had something they wanted to share with me.

At first I was worried that something bad had happened to them, so I contacted them right away. Turns out it was the lady from my tour who had taken the FB live video. She said once she posted it her kids kept messaging her asking who the man was in the mirror in the old timey costume. Recalling that there was no one in the bar fitting that description during our visit, I asked her to send me the picture.

She then related that the image appeared as the reflection of a person sitting at the bar. The clothes appeared to be from the mid to late 1800s. She said it was possible to run the video backwards and forwards and watch the apparition appear and disappear as she passed by the mirror in her video. As requested, she sent me both a still image and a snippet of the video, which played out exactly as she described. I'm including the still image for your examination.

Please note that the mirror is behind the main bar and is reflecting what is in front of it. There is a picture reflected in the mirror of a lady sitting on a chair. That is a famous E.J. Bellocq photograph of a Storyville prostitute. In the lower right hand corner, just below the Bellocq picture, you'll notice a slightly blurry image of a man in a smoking jacket, with a cravat, sitting with his elbow resting on the bar. That man was not there during our visit.

Was this a ghost, or perhaps a time slip, revealing the lingering spirit of a bygone patron hoping for one last adventure? We're not sure. Come join us for a visit and see for yourself.

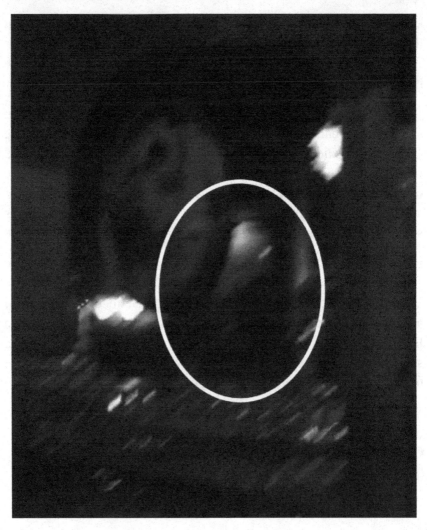

The mysterious man in the mirror

The next great capture happened a few months later after just telling my group about the ghost known as the Dancing Girl. A little girl who dances around the pool in a white dress. There one second, gone the next. Moments later one of our patrons caught this iridescent orb next to the pool at one of her favorite spots.

Orb of the Dancing Girl by the Pool

Still, one of my favorite tour experiences, ever, took place in this bar. And it wasn't even paranormal. I believe it was in the spring of 2017, I had an older kind of grizzled looking couple in my Pub Crawl tour group of 6 people. Picture the couple from the painting American Gothic. I was thoroughly convinced by the second stop on the tour that these people absolutely hated me.

I mean, it was kind of hard to miss, especially in that small of a group. They didn't laugh at any of my corny jokes, did respond to any of my creepy details. Nothing. Just stared at me with this cold hard look that made me think they were imagining my death in various Rob Zombie-esque back woods scenarios.

Once we got in May Baily's people scattered to the bathroom, or for drinks and I was alone at the corner of the bar. I turned to find the wife of the couple standing about three feet behind me. Silently staring. Yikes! She said "I want to ask you a question." And I thought, here it comes, she's going to tell me how much they hate the tour and ask for a refund. I said sure and she said "I need to tell you something about myself first. Then I'll ask." I said, okay.

Not sure what was coming next. She began to tell me about herself and how, as a much younger woman she had experienced a late term miscarriage. It was something that still haunted her. I felt everything in me soften at this point. She said that a few years after her miscarriage that a little girl in white, about maybe three or four years old, started showing up in her house. She was always laughing and smiling and playing. Then the lady stopped, looked me straight in the eye and asked "Do you think that could be my daughter?" I was floored. And speechless for a second. The breath caught in my throat.

Once I could breathe I responded with exactly what I felt and believe in my heart. "Ma'am, there are so many things that we don't know, or don't fully understand about this life. But from what I've seen and experienced, I think it's quite possible that she is your little girl. That she's showing you that she's okay, that you can let go of the guilt, and that you'll see each other again. I think it's important to her that you know that and that's why she lets you see her when she's happy."

She got teary eyed and hugged me. I got teary eyed, as well, and hugged her back. Then she pulled back, almost instantly composed and said "And here's the kicker. She even travels with us when we go to see relatives. I look up and there she is, in the corner of the living room or in our guest bedroom, where we're visiting. Ain't that the darndest thing?" I laughed and said, "It sure is. She's a part of the family and wants to be with you."

And that's when it hit me. For some people ghost stories are more than just fun tales and passing entertainment. For some, myself included, these are our stories. They speak to our essence, to our mortality and, also, to our hope for something after. So come for a visit to New Orleans and join us for an adventure. Who knows, one day we may just be telling people stories about you!

LOCAL HAUNTS

So now you've read our experiences, and we've loved sharing them with you. Now it's time to come out and have some of your own. To aid you in this quest we've put together a list of our favorite paranormal hot spots for you to check out. Happy hauntings!

BARS:

The Dragon's Den (435 Esplanade Ave.)

Reportedly the New Orleans home of occult priest Aleister Crowley in the early 1900's, this lovely dark corner of the city always seems to be exercising its demons. Great drinks and live music. And beware of the mirror on the second floor. It's said to be a portal to the other side.

The Dungeon (738 Toulouse St.)

My personal favorite in the French Quarter. Ashes of the dead in the courtyard planters, dark ambience and signature drinks. They even carry Marilyn Manson's own brand of Absinthe called Mansinthe. Distilled to 66.6 ABV, of course. Dance with spirits in the cage in the Sound Bar upstairs, hold captives at the Venus Bar or tempt fate by playing Zeppelin on the juke box downstairs. You never know who you may run into, living or dead.

Lafitte's Blacksmith Shop (941 Bourbon)

Purple Voodoo frozen daiquiris, pirate ghosts and candle lit interiors in the oldest existing bar in the United States hailing back to the late 1700's. What's not to love?

May Baily's (415 Dauphine St.)

A cornerstone of brothel history in the French Quarter with four active ghosts. Beautiful bar, live music and quite possibly the best Pimm's Cup in town. Get a courtyard room at the Dauphine Orleans for your best chance at a haunted encounter and tell Jen the bartender I said hello.

MRB (532 St. Phillip St.)

Wonderful bar with great drinks, an expansive courtyard and the ghost of a star-crossed and heartbroken prostitute who committed suicide in the late 1880's.

Pirate's Alley Café & Absinthe House (622 Pirate's Alley)

This lovely and inviting little corner of Pirate's Alley is brimming with atmosphere and history. The bartenders are experts on absinthe and you'll feel like you are being transported back to a time where anything was possible in this bustling old port city. For a price, of course. Pirate ghosts lurk in the alley by the Faulkner bookstore and echoes of the old jail whisper from the walls. The perfect place to wind down after a busy night of partying in the Quarter.

Santos (1135 Decatur St.)

High octane Goth rock metal bar on Lower Decatur with good drinks, live music and monthly Goth events. Even Phil Anselmo (Pantera) is known to show up with his band from time to time.

HOTELS:

Andrew Jackson Hotel (919 Royal St.)

Classic townhouse hotel with child ghosts and beautiful courtyard where they like to play.

Bourbon Orleans (717 Orleans Ave)

Situated smack in the middle of the French Quarter, this was our home base for all our visits. Nice accommodations, good food and a nice bar with live music. And, of course, several ghosts. Make sure you behave or else the Nun will get you.

The Dauphine Orleans Hotel (415 Dauphine St.)

Beautiful hotel set on an old brothel property from the late 1800's. Boasts four active spirits, especially in the pool and courtyard area by May Baily's, the hotel bar.

Lafitte Hotel & Bar (1003 Bourbon St.)

Located across from Lafitte's Blacksmith Shop Bar, this nicely appointed hotel is said to host the ghost of a grieving mother.

Lafitte Guest House (613 Esplanade Ave.)

Located on historic Esplanade Ave, which the Indians believed was a sacred path to the water, this quaint hotel is built upon mysterious tunnels that ran through the property in the 1800's and the ghost of a Lady in White, who inhabits room 6.

Lamothe House (621 Esplanade Ave.)

Built as a lavish residence in the 1800's by a wealthy sugar cane plantation owner, this property is occupied by the ghosts of a mother and her children along with a mysterious Lady in Red, who is believed to be one of the victims of a murder-suicide in the mid 1800's.

Hotel Monteleone (214 Royal St.)

A lavish family owned hotel that boasts its own spinning Carousel Bar, phantom children playing in the upper hallways and the ghost of a former employee, so dedicated, he refuses to leave. But you, you can check out any time you like.

Place D'Armes Hotel (625 St. Ann St.)

A very charming and welcoming hotel, centrally located near the original Place D'Armes (Jackson Square). Active spirits on the property include a chatty older gentleman with a beard who is believed to have been the head master at an old school formerly on the property.

Hotel Provincial (1024 Chartres St.)

Posh, family owned, boutique hotel located by the old Ursuline Convent. The ghosts of Confederate soldiers and hospital personnel are a few of the reported sightings on the property.

Villa Convento (621 Ursuline St.)

A lovely guest house with individually appointed rooms. Built in the 1830's it is rumored to have been a mid-19th century brothel, with active spirits seemingly from that era.

RESTAURANTS:

The Cornet Bar & Restaurant (700 Bourbon St.)

Creole cuisine with balconies overlooking Bourbon St. Named Cornet because the owning family, the Karnos, gave Louis Armstrong the money to purchase his first Cornet. Active hauntings include a mother and her two children who are believed to have perished in the devastating 1788 fire.

The Creole Cookery (514 Toulouse St.)

Classic creole and Cajun dishes with live jazz music in the courtyard, said to be the haunted end to a tragic love triangle in the early 1800's.

Muriel's Jackson Square (801 Chartres St.)

Fine dining in an exquisite location haunted by the ghost of a former owner who committed suicide after losing the property gambling. Ask to see the table they set out for him each evening and also the séance room upstairs. The crawfish and goat cheese crepes are a must!

Tableau (616 St. Peter)

With active ghosts from the Civil war era, a ghost cat and Psychic Medium dinner events this is a must attend haunted location. They even have a video on You Tube of wine bottles flying off the racks. Elegant dining in a historic building connected to the also haunted Le Petit Theatre on St. Peter St.

Tujague's (823 Decatur St.)

Legend has it that the original proprietors of this historic New Orleans restaurant, the Begues, were the folks credited with creating brunch. Serving traditional creole fare, it is a must for the discerning visitor and locals alike. The Sazeracs and Grasshoppers at the bar are outstanding. Several ghosts inhabit the property, including the still bickering Begues. The spirit of Julian Eltinge, a cross dressing actor from the silent film era, and frequent patron of the restaurant before he passed, is still believed to inhabit the building. For fun Goggle "Tujague's Ghost" to check out the images captured by patrons.

Turtle Bay (1119 Decatur St.)

A personal favorite. Fantastic burgers, steaks and a nice beer selection, in a casual setting. Their weekend crawfish boils, in season, are not to be missed. Active haunting on the property of a servant girl who died of yellow fever in the mid 1800's and the back courtyard was once the child cemetery off the back of the Ursuline Convent. Bon appetite!

STORY CONTRIBUTORS ~ YOUR GUIDES

DOUG BOOKOUT

A transplant to the city, I fell hard for this place during my first visit in 2004 and have never looked back. I believe that this is one of the few remaining places on earth where magic still exists.

I'm currently living out my retirement dream bucket list in the city that, thankfully, adopted me. After 36 years of military and Defense Industry career and family responsibilities, my wife and I decided to fast track our retirements while we were still young enough to enjoy everything this crazy town has to offer. My all-time absolute joy is sharing the city with people who get it and want to know more. You can find me most nights giving tours for Haunted History Tours and Jonathan Weiss Tours and working on various music projects with some of my favorite extremely talented people on the planet.

When I'm not doing that I'm hanging with my wife and best friend, Toni, and Chloe, the cutest and most spoiled puppy ever.

This book has been a labor of love and I sincerely hope you've enjoyed reading it as much as I have putting it together.

If I can help, in any way, to make your visit to the city more enjoyable, please contact me at:

deadfrenchmentour@facebook.com

or

Bookedout@cox.net

ARIADNE BLAYDE

Photo by Louis Maistros

Ariadne Blayde is a playwright and novelist. Her plays have been finalists for The Arts and Letters Prize, the Tennessee Williams Playwriting Contest, Lark Playwrights Week, and more. Her play "The Other Room" won the VSA Playwright Discovery Award and has had more than 300 productions around the world. An excerpt from her unpublished novel, ASH TUESDAY, was recently announced as a finalist for the 2020 Tennessee Williams Saints and Sinners Fiction Contest. Ariadne writes about New Orleans, social justice, and (at the moment) quantum physics. She moonlights as a ghost tour guide in the French Quarter.

More at **www.ariadneblayde.com**

DREW COTHERN

Drew Cothern is a New Orleans actor, entertainer and all around raconteur. You can catch him starring in Down's "Conjure" music video as well as other projects throughout the city.

Check out his art work and his on line store at:

Instagram.com@werewolvesofnola

www.redbubble.com/people/theunbeheld

CHARMAINE SWAN RICH

Charmaine was born and raised in New Orleans, LA. Her parents traced their French ancestry to the very beginnings of the city of New Orleans. The family tree includes a Major in the French army, Major Jean Fayard, who was assigned to New Orleans, and a "casket girl," named Angelique Girad – both arrived in New Orleans in the early 1720s.

Charmaine grew up in the Gentilly area of the city and the family moved across Lake Pontchartrain to Slidell, LA in the early 1980s. Attended Pope John Paul II High School and the University of New Orleans, graduating with a B.A. in Psychology and Sociology.

After graduation, she married her college sweetheart, a USMC officer. For the next 21 years they lived in ten different cities, too many deployments, a war, 2 children, 3 cats and 1 dog. Over the years and many different cities, she held jobs such as a school teacher, an athletic director, a coach, a financial advisor, a director of a at risk program for children, director of a child care center, a merchandiser for Macys, and substitute teacher.

Finally, retirement came for her husband, and home was calling. The family moved back to New Orleans in 2016. She became a tour guide in 2018. Currently the kids are in college and Charmaine has more time pursing her hobbies such as photography, jewelry making, flipping old furniture and, of course, ghost hunting. She loves being back in her hometown, and her favorite holiday is Mardi Gras. She is currently a member of the Krewe of Nyx, the Krewe of Morpheus and the Irish- Italian Club.

STELLA SALMEN

Stella is a Jersey Girl (now old lady) living in New Orleans since 2006. Always looking for the odd side of life, she has found it in the Crescent City working as a Bourbon Street Bartender, a Musician, and least favorite - a legal secretary. With each position she learned more about the city and the people who so proudly call it home.

With her love for interesting people, music, and history, it was only a matter of time before she became a Tour Guide, so that she could share her tales with the many visitors that descend upon the city every year.

SIDNEY SMITH

Sidney Smith is the owner of **Haunted History Tours,** New Orleans oldest and most popular tour company. *"My vision was to create a tour company in which tour guides possess enough acting ability and stage presence for their stories to leave each tour guest with a 'WOW!' experience."* Today Haunted History Tours employs over 40 tour guides offering several amazingly different tour options focusing mainly on the paranormal aspects of New Orleans intriguing past (and present).

Prior to creating *Haunted History,* Sidney was an active performer of singing telegrams and stripper grams for *Merry Minstrel Singing Telegrams*, an entertainment company he created in the late 1970's and sold in the early 1990's.

However, what put the owner of Haunted History Tours on the map early on, were his skills as a photographer of major rock stars. Sidney has worked directly with musicians such as Paul McCartney, the Rolling Stones, Led Zeppelin, Bruce Springsteen, Rod Stewart, Dr. John, and the Allman Brothers Band just to name a few. In 2019, for its 50th anniversary, he published a 256 page, hard cover, coffee table book, '70 - '74...Plus A Little Bit More / A Photographic Memoir On The Early Years of the Allman Brothers Band. To learn more, visit **www.AllmanBrothersBookBySidneySmith.com** or **www.RockStarPhotos.net**

Book Tours at: www.hauntedhistorytours.com

ROSE SINISTER

Photo by Tiffany Bailey

Rose Sinister is a ghost and vampire tour guide for Haunted History Tours in the French Quarter. Originally from Los Angeles, California, where she once pursued degrees in theater arts and anthropology, she dropped out of school and moved to New Orleans shortly after Hurricane Katrina, and never left.

She has since added the titles of "Podcaster" and "YouTuber" to her credentials, and you can find out more about her work on vampires and pop culture on her website, **rosesinister.com**

She currently resides in a haunted house with her husband, two derpy dogs, and a haughty black cat.

RANDY WALKER

Randy Walker is a fiction and creative non-fiction writer based out of New Orleans. He gives ghost tours in the French Quarter and basks in the inspirational insanity of his city. His writing has appeared in the magazines Stuff and Maxim and the online literary publications Neutrons Protons and Scarlet Leaf Review.

Check out Randy's good reads at: **Randythestoryteller.com**

JONATHAN WEISS

"I was first introduced to New Orleans in the flesh when I was but 7 years old. Wandering through the old streets, looking at sights I'd never imagined outside of a storybook, while I didn't have the experience to understand that I was looking at my home for the first time, I do remember that my thoughts were these: 'This place is magic. I will live here when I grow up.' Now, decades later, I've been fortunate to have seen this city in her many moods over the years."

Jonathan Weiss is one of the city's leading historians and purveyors of the macabre stories that makes New Orleans the most haunted city in America. Licensed two decades, he's one of the very, very few pre-Katrina guides still operating. Having lived in Boston, Philadelphia, Texas, Baltimore, D.C., Paris, and London among others, he still always returns home. Very few guides equal Jonathan in depth of experience, his knowledge of the old city and its neighborhoods, and in addition to his regular tours, he is able to accommodate private tours by request. Jonathan has appeared and consulted on The Vampire Diaries & The Originals, CMT, MTV, ATT Uverse, SyFy, Discovery, the Travel Channel, and for several films over the past decade, and most recently on William Shatner's "the UnXplained" on History.

For more info go to: **www.jonathanweisstours.com**

In 2020 I launched a new tour in concert with Jonathan Weiss Tours. Check it out!

Take a journey into an often unexplored area of the old city, and hear tales of the bones of the dead.

Explore the mystery of tunnels connecting to our dark past and walk the two most dangerous waterfront blocks in the world in the 1850's!

Learn the origin of Frenchmen Street and of the sacred energy that lured a satanic priest across the globe to perform rites in a property that still
requires rituals to keep the disquieted spirits at bay!
All of this and more awaits you on our

DARK HISTORY 2 - DEAD FRENCHMEN TOUR!

Available Thursday thru Sunday - 5 pm to 7 pm
Adults $25
Students/Teachers/Military/Seniors $18
Santos Bar - 1135 Decatur Street
To Book: JONATHANWEISSTOURS.COM
Or Call: (504) 681-9830
Like us on Facebook!